NOW WHAT?

Making the most
of your first forty days in Christ

Now What?
Making the most of your first forty days in Christ
© 2015

This book is dedicated to that crazy moment thousands of years ago in the Sinai when God led a guy named Abraham outside his tent, pointed to the starlit sky, and promised, "Look up at the heavens and count the stars—if indeed you can count them… So shall your offspring be.' Abraham believed God, and it was credited to him as righteousness." And so he became the father of all who believe. Think of it: Thousands of years later, you and I have become believers in Jesus. Which means—this is crazy—you and I are among the 'stars' Abraham tried to count that night. That promise was a prophecy with your name on it, so…

...welcome to your destiny.

INTRODUCTION

If you just made a fresh commitment to Jesus Christ, congratulations! We're celebrating with you. The first thing you need to know is this: *how you follow through in the next forty days is crucial.*

Research tells us it takes forty days to break old habits, and it takes about forty days to form new ones. I say this because the rhythm of your life is essentially a collection of habits—when and how you get up in the morning, your work and eating routines, your evening routines, and your bedtime rituals. For your faith to grow, you're going to have to make some important choices right away that will challenge dozens of your weekly habits.

Going to church on Sunday mornings from now on will mean changing some Saturday night habits—like when you get to bed. It will probably challenge how long you sleep in on Sunday morning, how long you linger over breakfast, and how much time you budget to make the kids presentable. It might change your lawn-mowing routine or when you do errands, and it might mean booking time off work when necessary.

Knowing how hard it is for old habits to change, I'd like you to pre-commit to three important things.

1. **Attend Manifest Mornings every Sunday.** If you wait until Sunday morning to decide whether you feel like going, the pull of your old habits is going to win out. If you plan ahead by blocking it off in your calendar and setting your alarm the night before, you're far more likely to follow through.

2. **Read one section in this book every day.** I've written this forty day experience to help you start the most important new habit of all—looking to Jesus for everything. Through it all, you'll start reading the Bible for yourself, too—which is way more important than this book is.

3. **Join a Life Group.** This will connect you with some great people on the same road you're on as you discover true life in Christ together. It may not work with your schedule at first if you've got prior commitments you need to ride out. But do it as soon as possible!

Well, that's it for now. Time to dive in! Next up: Day One.

What you'll be learning

What you'll be learning

DAY ONE
Welcome to the Family

Hey, how's it going?

I can only imagine how you must feel when it comes to this Jesus thing. You're probably thinking, *What just happened? What did I just do?*

On one hand, that's between you and God. I have no idea what's going on inside your head and heart.

But if you've been handed this book or picked it up for yourself, it's probably because you've made some sort of faith commitment to Jesus Christ and reading this book seemed like a logical next step to take.

I agree.

I wrote this stuff to walk you through your first forty days as a Believer in Jesus. Think of it as a crash course in your new life, complete with action steps to help make it real for you. So my best advice from here on in is this: *Don't just read it, do it. Try it.*

So what just happened to you? What did you just do? There are all kinds of ways to describe it. Maybe you:

- Put your faith in Jesus
- Gave your life to Jesus
- Invited Jesus into your life or heart
- Asked Jesus to forgive you for your sins
- Surrendered to Jesus
- Asked Jesus to save you and give you a new start
- Or maybe you'd describe it another way

The most important thing is to make sure you believe *God* sent his Son Jesus Christ *to do for you what you could never do for yourself—He died on the cross to pay for your sins, rescue you from your dead end life, and rose from the grave to give you new and eternal life with him.*

To make sure you've accepted his gift and made it personal, you could pray a prayer something like this:

"Jesus, I know I can't save myself or pay for my own sins. Thank you for dying on the cross to set me free. I accept your amazing gift and I'm looking forward to exploring my new life by following you from now on!"

There's a whole lot more to it than that, but that's the core idea. And it changes everything. One of Jesus' disciples, a guy named John, put it this way: "To everyone who received him, to all who believed in his name, he gave the right to become children of God" (John 1:12).

> You may be wondering why 'church writing' is peppered with quotes, brackets and numbers (like John 1:12). Those are quotes from the Bible. The first part (John) is the name of the book within the Bible the quote is found in. The numbers (1:12) refer to what chapter and verse is being quoted. So John 1:12 is from chapter one, verse twelve of the book of John. Don't worry, you'll learn more about the Bible as we go.

Back to what John wrote: "To everyone who received him, to all who believed in his name, he gave the right to become children of God" (John 1:12).

Your biggest problem was being separated from God; but now, through Jesus, you have full access to God forever! When you put your faith in Jesus, you became one of his children: "See what great love the Father has lavished on us, that we should be called children of God! And that is what we are!" (I John 3:1).

In other words, you were adopted into God's family forever. Jesus wants you to relate to God as your Father. Your heavenly Dad.

This is so important. The concept of 'God' can feel abstract and impersonal. "Father" is concrete, personal, and even emotional. All our human dads are deeply flawed and imperfect people—sometimes even abusive or absent. But Jesus wants you to imagine God as the perfect Father we all long to have—always present and engaged with you, unconditionally loving, endlessly patient, all-powerful, and never failing.

Embracing God as your father and relating to him as his child changes prayer: You're a child talking to a Father who adores you, not just a speck of dust calling out to some distant divine Being.

This also changes how you see your place in the world: You are loved and accepted, totally secure because your Father is always with you.

It also changes how you see 'church'—these are your brothers and sisters in Jesus. We're all a little bit messed up, but we're all unconditionally loved by our heavenly Dad. When this dawns on you, you'll be changed forever, and you'll want everyone on earth to experience the same love you've been given.

NOW... RESPOND

Jesus says, "When you pray, say, "Father." Or "Dad." Or "Daddy." So now it's time to try try it by actually praying. Don't try and sound religious or smart. Just talk to him.

It could even be, "Uh, hi Dad. It's me..." and then thank him for what he's done for you so far.

Seriously. Don't skip this. Talk to your dad. Tell him how you're doing, what you're wondering, what you need help with. He's listening, and just like a loving parent, he's thrilled that you want to talk to him. Talk to him any time, and about everything.

Have fun, and see you tomorrow!

7

DAY TWO
Initiative and Response

Congratulations, you made it to day two in your new life with Jesus!

Have you been talking to our Father in heaven? How's it been going? If it feels awkward at first, don't worry. It'll become normal before you know it.

What I want you to know today is, *Christianity is not a religion*. A lot of people think so and live like it, but faith in Christ wasn't meant to be a system. It's a relationship with a God who becomes our Father through faith in Jesus.

The essence of religion is this: *You initiate, God responds*. You work and strive to please God, trying to press him to respond to you with love, pardon, blessing… whatever you need him for. And there are strict rules about how it all works.

Christian faith says the opposite: God (through Christ) has done the work—and invites you to respond to *him* by faith. He wants you to accept the work he did for you and love him back.

The good news is that Jesus *has* done, *is* doing, and *will do* all the things you can't do for yourself. And he offers them to you for free, as you confess your inability to achieve them and simply receive them by faith. As you respond to him.

To receive the new things Jesus is teaching you, you'll need to do something the Bible calls *repenting*. Repentance is a way of describing how you let go of your old way of life and thinking so you can believe and embrace the new way in Jesus.

The Apostle Paul, one of Jesus' early followers (who wrote a good chunk of the New Testament) encouraged people to think of God's initiative and their responding this way:

> "I pray that you, being rooted and established in (God's) love, may have power, together with all the Lord's holy people, to grasp how wide and long and high and deep is the love of Christ, and to know this love that surpasses knowledge—that you may be filled to the measure of all the fullness of God" (Ephesians 3:17-19).

In other words, you are now like a plant with roots growing deeper every day into the unfathomable love of God. Your life is about drinking in God's love. As you respond to him, your life on the outside will grow to look more and more like the love that fills you on the inside.

You don't have to make it all work. You don't have to change yourself or become some kind of 'super-christian' by next Sunday. He'll take care of changing your life. All you need to do is become attentive to what God is doing or saying, and respond—as a way of life. Be sure to get yourself to church every week, to hang out with fellow plants learning to live in God's love like you are.

If something needs to change in your life, repent. Ask God to help you let go of the old way of thinking. And then accept the new truth and start living it out. That's obeying God, and it's one of the ways we love him back.

NOW... RESPOND

How do you sense God wants you to respond to him right now? Maybe... by thanking him? Asking him questions? Praying about something in your life? Do what you sense him asking you to do. And when he talks to you about your old ways of thinking, speaking, acting, choosing, spending... remember, all he wants is for you to respond with faith and love.

DAY THREE
Growing up

Guess what? The new life you've been given in Jesus is so radical, it's called being "born again" (John 3:3,7)! You started your new life in God's spiritual family as a newborn. It's not an insult; it just means you're brand-new at this faith thing. That's not just okay, it's *normal.*

This is why the Apostle Peter, another disciple of Jesus, wrote, "Like newborn babies, crave pure spiritual milk, so that by it you may grow up in your salvation, now that you have tasted that the Lord is good" (I Peter 2:2). The New Testament also mentions several other spiritual life stages: *children, young men/women,* and *adults/parents.*

The idea is this: We all begin as spiritual newborns, but God expects you to grow up in the faith and become mature in Christ—just like we expect our babies to grow up and become mature, productive adults. And you'll grow up spiritually much like you do physically: Step by step, gradually building on skills, coordination, and what you learn over time.

Right now, you don't know very much about God or how this Jesus thing works. You don't know how to read the Bible and 'feed' yourself spiritually. You're not very confident praying. You're not sure how to walk out a lot of the things the other Christians around you are doing. But like a newborn eager to take on the world, you'll learn. You'll grow. You'll mature as you commit to follow Jesus through all of life.

The verse I quoted above said that we should crave *spiritual milk* to nourish ourselves spiritually. Newborns don't eat solid food because they can't chew it and digest it themselves. That's what this book is for: I'm helping you digest simple spiritual food (milk) so you can grow up in your faith. As you mature, you'll learn to chew, swallow and digest the truths of the Bible for yourself. When you regularly feed and take care of yourself spiritually, you'll know you're growing up in your faith.

Right now you're a newborn Believer. A newborn doesn't know how to survive on it's own and couldn't if it tried. You need a spiritual family around you to help you survive in your faith and grow up in Jesus.

For starters, commit to attending Manifest Mornings. But for the true 'family experience,' you should also join a Manifest Life Group. Life Groups are smaller groups of Believers who connect during the week to help each other discover true life in Christ. When Christianity began, the heart of the movement was this kind of family:

"They devoted themselves to the apostles' teaching and to fellowship, to the breaking of bread and to prayer. Everyone was filled with awe at the many wonders and signs performed by the apostles. All the believers were together and had everything in common. They sold property and possessions to give to anyone who had need. Every day they continued to meet together in the temple courts. They broke bread in their homes and ate together with glad and sincere hearts." (Acts 2:42-45).

NOW... RESPOND

Take some time to ponder what you learned in today's reading. What stood out to you, and why? Talk to God about that and ask him what you need to do about it. Then do it.

I realize it may feel a bit scary, but if you aren't part of a Life Group yet, take this step and join one. You'll be glad you did. You can find current information about Life Groups at the Welcome Centre on a Manifest Morning or through the Manifest Church mobile App, available in the Apple and Google App Stores.

DAY FOUR
Approval

Now that you've got a few simple Bible concepts under your belt (congratulations, by the way) it's time to dive into *what Jesus has done for you*. It's going to blow your mind.

> * The writers of the Bible call what Jesus did for us "the good news" or "the gospel" (which means the same thing). So next time when you hear those words, you'll know what they're referring to. You're welcome!

The Apostle Paul describes us from God's perspective, and it's not pretty. He says we're all "alike... under the power of sin... There is no one righteous, not even one... for all have sinned and fall short of the glory of God" (Romans 3:9,10,23). Sin is falling short of God's glory—his own perfect character and ideal life for us. Bottom line, Jesus would not have come to die a horrible death for us if we'd been doing just fine on our own. Humanity needed more than help; we needed a rescue.

Despite our best efforts we're all unrighteous, which is just what it sounds like: *Un-right. We're not right*, living in conflict with God and each other. Sin hurts us and the world around us.

Our lies destroy trust. Our violence injures and kills. our greed robs the less fortunate and corrupts our own hearts. Our adultery shatters families. Our pride excludes others. On and on it goes.

Here's the thing: God loves you too much to let the people who've hurt you off the hook without justice. But God also loves *others* too much to let *you* off the hook when you hurt *them* (and hurt yourself!). In other words, God can't ignore sin in you or anyone else. He's both too holy and too loving to let it go. This means that without Jesus, we all stand guilty and unrighteous before God, deserving of condemnation and eternal punishment (Romans 6:23).

But "God so loved the world"—that's you and me—"that he gave his one and only Son, so that whoever believes in him would not perish but have everlasting life" (John 3:16). When you put your faith in Jesus, you're united with him and reap the benefits of his amazing, eternal life—all the astounding things he is, did, and does.

So Jesus, who was fully God and fully human, came and lived among us on earth. He lived the perfect life we could never live, measuring up to God's glorious ideal, holy and righteous like we could never be. This perfect One, Jesus, took all the sin of the world on his shoulders on the cross, and he did it for you.

And now, because you've put your faith in him, you reap the benefits of his righteousness: "He who knew no sin (Jesus) was made to be sin on our behalf, so that we might become the righteousness of God" (I Corinthians 5:21). In other words, *Jesus lived the perfect life you could never live and gave you the credit for it.*

This means God has declared you righteous in Christ. It means "there is now no condemnation for those who are in Christ Jesus... If God is for us, who can be against us?... Who will bring any charge against those whom God has chosen? It is God who justifies. Who then is the one who condemns? No one!" (Romans 8:1,31,33,34).

Let that sink in: Because of Jesus, you have the final approval of the God of the universe. Who cares what anyone else thinks? This means you can be from living to gain the approval of people around you. It means you don't have to fear their disapproval. You stand justified before God and the world can't touch it.

Because this approval came from Jesus and his work is already accomplished, it can't be taken from you. Your approval isn't dependent on your performance or your track record. Nothing you can do will change it. It's a gift, a given, ready for you to bite into and enjoy now and forever!

> Because of Jesus, you have the final approval of the God of the universe. Who cares what anyone else thinks?

Think of how much energy you spend trying to validate or prove yourself—to God, to people, or even yourself. What would it be like to never need that approval ever again, because you've already got all the approval you'll ever need? Think of the ongoing pressure you feel to perform, to succeed, to come through. What would it be like to let your soul off the treadmill of perfectionism, knowing you don't have to be perfect because Jesus is already perfect for you?

Can you see how amazing this is? You don't have to try and impress the Christians you've just met or pretend to have it all together. They're a mess too, just like you are. Jesus is the perfect One, not you. Not them. We get to be human!

And think of people who don't know Jesus yet: The friend trying to prove themselves to their new boss, the hyper-driven athlete trying to live up to an unrealistic body image, the mother who always thinks she's failing and falling short as a parent. Can you see how they need this gift from Jesus too, and how refreshing it would be for them to find his approval?

Lots to think about, I know. These truths you're learning are the foundation of your new life in Christ.

NOW... RESPOND

Try praying a prayer like this one in response:

Father, all my life I've tried to prove myself and gain the approval of others, but that's endless and exhausting. Jesus, thank-you for living the perfect life I could never live and giving me the credit for it. Thank-you that I'm totally accepted now and set right in your eyes because of Jesus' gift. Thank you that my standing with you isn't based on how good I am at this faith thing. Help me to live under the smile of your approval, free from all condemnation now and forever!

DAY FIVE
Loved and Forgiven

How are you doing? Feeling overwhelmed, maybe? Maybe you forgot to read this book for a few days. No worries! You've got your whole life to grow up into the person God wants you to be. Remember, the most important thing is that God initiates all the important stuff, and your job is just to respond by trusting him. As you read this book, God will speak to you. As you listen, he'll help you respond to his work in your life.

Yesterday you learned that Jesus lived the perfect life you could never live and gives you the credit for it. This frees you from the endless pressure to prove yourself—to God or anyone else. You have his approval, period.

You've also been learning that God sent Jesus to rescue us because he loves us. And it's true! Wherever Jesus went, he loved people and helped them with their struggles. He fed the hungry, hugged the un-huggable, stood up for the oppressed, healed the sick, raised the dead, ate with the lonely, forgave the sinners, and gave hope to the hopeless.

God shows his love every time he heals your body of sickness. He shows his love by putting people in your life who care about you and take care of you. He shows his love with every sunset and summer shower that helps the plants grow. He shows his love with each answered prayer and during the times when we sense his presence with us. His love really is expressed in a million ways, a million times a day.

As amazing as those things are, though, the Apostle Paul says that "God demonstrates his own love for us in this: While we were still sinners, Christ died for us" (Romans 5:8). Isaiah tells us that on the cross, Jesus bore the full weight of all our pain, all our darkness, all our sickness, sadness, suffering, sin, and the punishing death we deserve to die for our own sins (Isaiah 53:4,5). His infinitely precious blood paid for your forgiveness now and forever. "We have been made holy through the sacrifice of the body of Jesus Christ once for all" (Hebrews 10:10).

Jesus did this for you more than two thousand years ago, in advance—pre-paying for every sin you'd ever commit because he loves you. This proves his love for you *once and for all*. You are perfectly and permanently loved and accepted by God, totally forgiven and free from all guilt and shame for ever!

Great news—from now on, you're free from having to please others or earn their love and acceptance. You don't have to 'suck up' to God, pay off your sins, earn his love, or make things up to him. And because he just plain loves you, knowing full well what you've done, are doing, and will do in the future,

> "I am convinced that neither death nor life, neither angels nor demons, neither the present nor the future, nor any powers, neither height nor depth, nor anything else in all creation, will be able to separate us from the love of God that is in Christ Jesus our Lord" (Romans 8:38,39).

When others reject or judge you, you're still loved. When people get mad at you or hate you, you're still loved. When you feel unlovable, you're still loved. When you blow it and are unworthy of love, you're still loved by God. There's nothing you can do about it… but accept it, enjoy it, and live in it.

NOW… RESPOND

Wow, right?

Reading what you just read, drinking it in… how do you want to respond to God? Tell him what you're thinking, how it makes you feel to know you're loved unconditionally and forever by him. Thank him, praise him, and ask him to help you live in his love from now on.

DAY SIX
Alive and Then Some

Let's review.

When you put your faith in Jesus, you became a child of God, which means he's now your Father in heaven—and other Believers are now your spiritual family.

You were saved because God took the initiative to reach out to save you. Your job, as it will be from now on, was simply to respond by believing him. Trusting him.

You began your life in Christ as a spiritual newborn. With the help of your spiritual family and regular Bible teaching to feed on, you'll grow up in your faith.

As we put our faith in Christ, we reap the benefits of the work he did for us. For starters, Jesus came and lived the perfect life we could never live and gives us the credit for it. Because we're approved by God, we don't have to live to prove ourselves or live for others' approval ever again.

Jesus proved God's love for us by dying on the cross to pay for our sins. Through him we get total forgiveness, a new start, and the unconditional love of God forever. We don't have to live to please others or work to pay for our sins anymore.

As you can see, the life Jesus lived *two-thousand years ago* is the good news we live by *today*. But it gets even better! Jesus rose from the grave, defeating death, sin, and the power of the devil—all in one blow:

"He… shared in (our) humanity so that by his death he might break the power of him who holds the power of death—that is, the devil." (Hebrews 2:14)

"God raised him from the dead, freeing him from the agony of death, because it was impossible for death to keep its hold on him" (Acts 2:24)

"Since Christ was raised from the dead, he cannot die again; death no longer has mastery over him. The death he died, he died to sin once for all; but the life he lives, he lives to God." (Romans 6:9,10).

Because you trust Jesus, you receive the benefits of what he accomplished. Paul says there is:

> "incomparably great power for us who believe. That power is the same as the mighty strength he exerted when he raised Christ from the dead and seated him at his right hand in the heavenly realms, far above all rule and authority, power and dominion, and every name that is invoked, not only in the present age but also in the one to come." (Ephesians 1:18-21).

> "Just as Christ was raised from the dead through the glory of the Father, we too may live a new life. For if we have been united with him in a death like his, we will certainly also be united with him in a resurrection like his. For we know that our old self was crucified with him so that the body ruled by sin might be done away with... if we died with Christ, we believe that we will also live with him." (Romans 6:4-8)

The benefits you receive from Jesus' resurrection are astounding:

- You never need to fear death, because even when your body dies, you'll live forever.
- You don't have to produce your own success and be in control of your life, because you share access to the same power that raised Jesus from the dead (Ephesians 1:19,20).
- You've been freed from the power of sin, which means you can break free from unhealthy patterns and habits in your life.
- You share Jesus' victory over the devil and his demons, including all their schemes to oppose your new faith.

NOW... RESPOND

By now you've probably noticed there is a giant gap between what Jesus has given you and how much of that you've experienced so far. Every Believer struggles with this! God has done the work for us through Jesus; we just have to learn how to receive it on a practical level.

One of the Bible verses I quoted above is part of a prayer Paul would pray for his fellow Believers. Try praying it out loud for yourself:

Glorious Father, please give me the Spirit of wisdom and revelation, so that I can know You better. May the eyes of my heart be enlightened so I can know the hope to which You have called me, the riches of Your glorious inheritance in his spiritual family, and Your incomparably great power for me because I believe. That power is the same as the mighty strength You exerted when You raised Christ from the dead and seated him at Your right hand in the heavenly realms, far above all rule and authority, power and dominion, and every name that is invoked, not only in the present age but also in the one to come.

People all around you are struggling to make life work on their own strength. They're afraid of death and the afterlife. They feel like they need to be in control of their lives and and are anxious about what might happen to them. You know someone in your world who needs Jesus and what he's done. Pray for them, and look for an opportunity to share what Jesus has done for you with them.

DAY SEVEN
The Holy Spirit

After Jesus rose from the dead, he kept appearing to his disciples over a period of forty days, teaching and encouraging them. One day, he said,

> "Do not leave Jerusalem, but wait for the gift my Father promised, which you have heard me speak about... in a few days you will be baptized with the Holy Spirit... you will receive power when the Holy Spirit comes on you; and you will be my witnesses in Jerusalem, and in all Judea and Samaria, and to the ends of the earth." After he said this, he was taken up before their very eyes..." (Acts 1:3-5,8,9).

In other words, Jesus left the earth, ascending to take his place back to his rightful throne in heaven. But don't worry, Jesus said: "I won't leave you as orphans. I will come to you." How? By sending his Spirit.

> * How do God, Jesus, the Father, and the Holy Spirit fit together? We'll never truly understand it—but "there is one God" (I Timothy 2:5)... made up of three distinct Persons (Father, Son, and Holy Spirit). We've call this three-in-one mystery the *Trinity*. There are Bible verses that say the Father is God (I Peter 1:2), that Jesus is God (John 1:1,14), that the Spirit is God (Luke 1:35), and verses that refer to all three at one time (Matthew 28:18-20). Most verses in the New Testament referring to God in general are about *the Father* unless they say otherwise.

When you became a Believer in Jesus, he sent his Spirit to be with you and live in you forever (John 14:17,18). Through the Holy Spirit, God manifests Jesus in us, filling our hearts with his love and unlocking the limitless potential of heaven for us to access as we serve him and love others (Ephesians 3:16-21).

This is why almost every reading in this book includes three angles:

- What this means for you personally—your connection to God
- What this means for your relationships with other Believers
- What this can mean for people in your life that haven't put their faith in Jesus yet.

Lock into that triad: *Me, us, the rest of the world.* The Holy Spirit isn't just for you. The Father sent Jesus to be with us on earth and rescue us. Jesus sent the Spirit to be in our hearts so he could fill us with himself. And the Spirit sends us (the family of God) into the world, equipped with his power so we can help more and more people discover true life in Christ like we have.

Welcome to God's family, a family on a mission to manifest Jesus! Church isn't for church people; it's for the world Jesus died to save. He sent his Spirit to make sure we have what we need to finish the mission he started. Consider this your official commissioning. You are now a missionary! Whenever you see people around you pursuing lesser things they think will satisfy them, you know they need the Holy Spirit.

The Holy Spirit is the One who applies what Jesus did *for* you and brings it to life *in* you. His presence within you makes you a brand new person, an amazing new creation. This new creation is the new you, the real you. Because of the Holy Spirit empowering this new self, you can live a new life.

Paul says the new, real you "is created to be like God in true righteousness and holiness" (Ephesians 4:22). He also says your new self is "being renewed in knowledge in the image of it's creator" (Colossians 3:10).

The old you, your "sinful nature," was crucified with Christ. The problem is, that old you is all you know. You're used to thinking those old thoughts, keeping those old habits, using those same old destructive attitudes. So you'll bump into that old way of living life every single day. Paul's advice is, "Put to death, therefore, whatever belongs to your earthly (old) nature" (Colossians 3:5). Why? Because that's not you anymore. The new you is a gift from God, and it's awesome.

NOW... RESPOND

Instead of me writing out your prayer today, make one up on your own, putting some of the things you learned today into words.

- Thank him for the Holy Spirit, that Jesus lives inside you now. Ask the Holy Spirit to fill you with power to live from your new self in Christ
- Who in your world do you think God is sending you to love and reach out to? Talk to God about them!
- Ask the Holy Spirit to work through you with his power as you live your life this week.

DAY EIGHT
Mission Accomplished

From the moment sin entered the world through human disobedience, life has been screwed up in every way. Sin unleashed endless corruption, sickness, conflict, pain, sadness, and the ongoing horror of death (Romans 5:12). You and I don't know any different, but God remembers what life was like before this "fall" and it's been his highest mission to restore what was lost ever since.

In heaven, all the perfection and glory of God's original kingdom design are still intact, radiant and brimming with life. Jesus came to earth bearing the life and power of heaven, bent on sharing it with whoever would receive him. His mission was and is manifesting pieces of heaven on earth.

"This, then, is how you should pray," Jesus explained. "Our father in heaven, hallowed be your name, your kingdom come, your will be done, on earth as it is in heaven" (Matthew 6:9,10). God's will is that his kingdom would come on earth just like it is in heaven. This is what prayer is about—manifesting the kingdom of heaven—and it's also how he taught us to live.

Jesus' death and resurrection unleashed powerful potential to manifest glimpses this kingdom here and now. Everyone who repents of their sin and puts their faith in him becomes a kingdom-bearer like Jesus was.

> The mission is manifesting heaven on earth.

When he sent his disciples out to spread his message, he told them, "As you go, proclaim this message: 'The kingdom of heaven has come near.' Heal the sick, raise the dead, cleanse those who have leprosy, drive out demons. Freely you have received; freely give" (Matthew 10:7,8). As you learned yesterday, when Jesus ascended into heaven he sent his Spirit to be with us and within us to help us complete this mission.

This doesn't mean heaven will manifest itself perfectly here and now. It doesn't mean all darkness and death will be banished by our faith in Jesus in this lifetime. It doesn't mean every sick person will get healed (even though this is God's "on earth as it is in heaven" will).

Painfully, we now live in an in-between time where "all of creation has been groaning, as in the pains of childbirth," longing with us for the day when the kingdom will fully manifest—when heaven will finally invade earth and wipe away all sin and death forever (Romans 8:22). In the meantime, because Jesus defeated death, he says, "Do not let your hearts be troubled... My Father's house has many rooms... I am going there to prepare a place for you... And if I go and prepare a place for you, I will come back and take you to be with me that you also may be where I am" (John 14:1-3). An eternity with Jesus in heaven awaits us:

> "In his great mercy he has given us new birth into a living hope through the resurrection of Jesus Christ from the dead, and into an inheritance that can never perish, spoil or fade. This inheritance is kept in heaven for you, who through faith are shielded by God's power until the coming of the salvation that is ready to be revealed in the last time" (I Peter 1:3-5).

Your calling is to live and pray for God's kingdom to come as much as possible here and now. But even when you don't see heaven's glorious ideal manifest in your life (yet), you can know beyond a shadow of a doubt that it will be one day—and that it will totally be worth the wait.

Human beings tend to live with a subtle pressure to make the most of this life... or else. If this life is all there is, we can take one of two approaches. Either we party hard or we work hard, knowing this is our one and only shot to enjoy the good things in life. The clock is ticking, after all, counting down to the last day of our lives.

But if this life is not all there is, and if the best really is yet to come for Believers like us, then the pressure's off!

We can both work and enjoy life without demanding everything work out for us. We can give people grace when they inadvertently ruin special moments or rob us of happiness through their own quest for meaning and fulfillment. If we don't get around to our bucket lists we can smile inside knowing that far greater joy awaits us in heaven.

And in heaven, by the way, the clock isn't counting down. It's counting up... and will never stop.

That's the kind of freedom people all around you are desperate for but

---

* You may have friends and family who, to the best of your knowledge, never became Believers in Jesus before they died. Are they in hell? The truth is, we can't know for sure where they stood with God before they died. The best plan is to trust our loving and perfectly just Father to handle those issues and focus on the people we still have with us.

can't have—because without Jesus, the clock really is ticking. Whoever hasn't trusted him as Rescuer and Master before they die will spend eternity suffering in hell without him (II Corinthians 5:10, Revelation 21:11-15). When you see people struggling with the ticking clock in their lives, be bold. Take a moment to share what Jesus has done for you and how a new peace is replacing the old pressures and anxiety.

NOW... RESPOND

Okay, what do you need to thank God for? Do it now!

Next, there are probably things in your life that you still feel like "now or never" issues. You're stressed over things that don't stack up when compared to eternal realities like we've been discussing. Confess that to God, receive his forgiveness, and ask him to convince you of his good news instead.

What about people in your life who don't know Jesus yet? Pray for them, and pray for chances to plant little truths about Jesus for them to think about.

DAY NINE

Completeness

If you can even begin to grasp what I'm going to share with you today, it will change everything else you do from now on.

Let's review. As you trust Jesus, you get all the credit and benefits from the work he did on your behalf:

Jesus lived the perfect life you could never live, and has now given you his full approval. You never have to prove yourself—ever again.

Jesus died in your place to pay for sins you could never pay for, restoring the broken relationship with God you could never fix. This proves his love and acceptance of you both now and forever. You are unconditionally loved, accepted, and forgiven by the King of the Universe.

Jesus rose from the dead, defeating the ultimate enemies you could never defeat on your own—death and the devil. In him, you will now live forever and share his cosmic authority over the devil and all his demons. You are victorious because of his power and never have to fear failure, evil, or death.

Jesus sent his Spirit to be with you and in you forever, embodying his presence and power within you and commissioning you to help him manifest heaven on earth. You never have to pursue lesser thrills to fill your soul because he is all you need from now on.

> As you trust Jesus, you get all the credit and benefits from the work he did on your behalf.

Jesus went to prepare an eternal home for you, so you are secure in him forever.

All this prompted Peter, one of Jesus' original twelve disciples, to write, "His divine power has given us everything we need for a godly life through our knowledge of him" (II Peter 1:3).

Paul, an early champion of Christianity, said much the same thing: "Praise be to the God and Father of our Lord Jesus Christ, who has blessed us in the heavenly realms with every spiritual blessing in Christ" (Ephesians 1:3).

He later expressed it this way: "For in Christ all the fullness of the Deity lives in bodily form, and in Christ you have been brought to fullness" (Colossians 2:9).

So you may *feel* rejected, but you're accepted.

You might *feel* like a failure, but you're more than a conquerer.

You might *feel* alone, but the Holy Spirit is with you and in you.

You might *feel* unloved, but Jesus loved you so much he died for you.

You might *feel* worthless, but he thought you were worth dying for.

You might *feel* aimless, but you have the greatest mission in the universe.

You might *feel* empty, but you are overflowing with Jesus.

You might *feel* unworthy or disqualified, but Jesus has qualified you.

You might *feel* useless, but you have an important role to play in Christ's family.

Every emotional and spiritual need you have has already been met by Jesus. The gap between what you experience and what Jesus has offered can only be bridged by faith, as you learn to reject what feels true and embrace what God says instead. Don't let your feelings define your reality; let Jesus define your world instead.

Other Believers struggle with this stuff too, don't worry. But the more you believe what God says about you, the more peace and joy you'll feel. We're in this together, remember?

And this is good news! The empty, aimless, insecure, lonely people around you need Jesus, and you can help point the way.

NOW... RESPOND

Today, you'll experience a whole bunch of the old emotions, trying to make you feel worthless, aimless, empty, insecure, threatened, and more. Now you know what's going on. Now you can look to Jesus and say, "No. I don't want this. Jesus, thank you that I am accepted, loved, and secure. Holy Spirit, please convince me of this fact. Amen."

DAY TEN
Making Jesus Your Way

If you're a Believer in Jesus then you've become one of his disciples (his apprentice), someone who follows their Master because they want to become like them.

Jesus put it this way: "I am the Way, the Truth, and the Life. No one comes to the Father except through me" (John 14:6). So following Jesus means making him your Way, your Truth, and your Life.

None of us really like being told how to do things. In fact, one way of describing what the insult "Go to hell" means is telling someone 'where to go and how to get there.' "Don't tell me how to live my life!" is our typical response to unwanted opinions about how we do things even if we know we need help and direction.

We try so hard to convince ourselves we don't need other people's input. We'll figure things out on our own, right? And then we spend hours every week Googling how to do things, reading online reviews (made up of regular people's opinions) and pinning DIY projects we couldn't have figured out how to on our own.

Making Jesus your Way means letting the One who lived the perfect life, died in your place to set you free, defeated death, sin, and the devil, sent the Holy Spirit to empower you, and is Lord of the afterlife… tell you how to live your life. The *way* he offers is the *how-to* you so desperately need.

In *Day Two* we touched on the fact that faith in Jesus means responding to his initiative vs initiating and trying to get him to respond to you. Making Jesus your Way takes things a step further. Jesus puts it like this:

> "I am the vine; you are the branches. If you remain in me and I in you, you will bear much fruit; apart from me you can do nothing" (John 15:5)

Apart from Jesus, you can't do his will. Remember? *His kingdom come, his will be done, on earth as it is in heaven.*

His will for you isn't just that you'd be a good parent; it's that through you, your kids would taste a bit of heaven's life and power. His will isn't just for you to be a good employee; it's that through your work, people would get a supernatural glimpse of God's goodness. You can't do that on your own strength. Neither can I!

Making Jesus your Way means adopting an *"I can't do it, Jesus, but you can through me"* posture as a way of life. Jesus was your only Way to the Father and salvation, and he's your only Way to do the will of the Father from now on. What you need—what we all need—is to spend time with other people learning to make Jesus their Way just like we are. If you haven't joined a Life Group yet, pick one and dive in!

King Solomon wrote that "there is a way that seems right but in the end, it leads to death" (Proverbs 16:25). All around you people are making a go of life their own way—and it seems to to be working for the most part.

But only Jesus' way can deliver true life both on earth and for eternity. When people's lives crumble, they're typically more open to input. Watch for moments like those, where you can lovingly step in and share what Jesus' Way has done for you. Their eternal destiny may depend on it.

> Making Jesus your Way means adopting an *"I can't do it, but you can through me"* posture as a way of life.

NOW... RESPOND

Have you ever thought of God's will as being more than being a 'good' parent/spouse/friend/employee? Talk to God about that. And then listen. What does it seem like he's asking you to do about it? What would it look like to depend on him for everything in your life?

DAY ELEVEN
Making Jesus Your Truth

We live in a world that's lost it's grip on truth.

During his fateful trial before Pontius Pilate, Jesus declared, "The reason I was born and came into the world is to testify to the truth. Everyone on the side of truth listens to me" (John 18:37).

"What is truth?" Pilate replied. On one level, it's a fair question. But it's also a copout.

Much of our modern thought was based on Rene Descartes' maxim, "I think, therefore I am." Our culture has replaced Descartes idea with another maxim: "I feel, therefore I am." If someone feels like a woman, they're apparently a woman now. If a caucasian feels black, then apparently they're black. If we feel like leaving our spouse because the new guy feels right, we can go for it. Apparently.

People squirm when we talk about truth because if objective truth exists, we're accountable to it—and we'd rather not be. Jesus, as usual, nails it on the head: "Everyone who does evil hates the light, and will not come into the light for fear that their deeds will be exposed"(John 3:20). The truth hurts.

When Pilate asked, "What is truth?" it was an attempt to avoid responsibility. As Lev Grossman has said, "There is no event so plain and clear that a determined human being can't find ambiguity in it."

In contrast, Webster's dictionary says a synonym for truth is *reality*. Truth doesn't describe how I *feel* about a thing; it describes the thing *itself*. It describes reality.

So... when Jesus says, "I am the Truth," he's saying he's the embodiment of reality itself; that when he speaks, he's describing the world as it really is and how it really works—more clearly and more accurately than we've ever heard before or will ever hear again. To reject his take on things is, quite simply, to choose to live in a fantasy world. Jesus isn't just nice, he's *right*. Every time.

Better let that sink in. While you're at it, chew on these ideas:

- Your feelings are not the same as truth.
- Your feelings are based on your perception of reality. They're not reality itself.
- The strength of a feeling has nothing to do with how true it is.

- Your feelings can tell you what track you're on, but not whether you're on the right track in the first place.

To make Jesus your Truth means you've decided to let Jesus define your reality. When your feelings (or even your best thinking) conflicts with what Jesus says is true, you go with Jesus. Even if the whole world sees reality a different way, you go with Jesus. And it will happen! Once, after Jesus said some particularly difficult things,

> "...many of his disciples turned back and no longer followed him. "You do not want to leave too, do you?" Jesus asked the Twelve. Simon Peter answered him, "Lord, to whom shall we go? You have the words of eternal life. We have come to believe and to know that you are the Holy One of God" (John 6:66-69).

This is also why I keep encouraging you to join a Life Group and dive right in to the Bible Studies. The Bible is God's truth in written form. You need a 'family' of disciples around you learning to live in the reality Jesus describes. It's also why we need to share the truth with people who don't know Jesus yet: they're living in a fantasy world we know can't bring them full and eternal life like Jesus offers.

> To make Jesus your Truth means you've decided to let him define your reality.

NOW... RESPOND

Have you been struggling with something you're learning as a new Believer because it conflicts with what you thought was true all your life? Probably, right?

Take a few minutes to confess that to God. Tell him you're choosing to make him your ultimate Truth, and ask him to keep changing your perspective to match his so you can live the life he wants for you.

DAY TWELVE
Making Jesus Your Life

The past few days I've been getting you to chew on a really important Bible verse (John 14:6), when Jesus said, "I am the Way, the Truth, and the Life; no one comes to the Father except through me." I said that to follow Jesus means learning to make him *your* Way, *your* Truth, and *your* Life.

What does it mean to make Jesus your Life?

You don't just get life, or even a life-style; you get Jesus. He is the Life you've been longing for, the Source of everything your soul truly craves. As your relationship with him grows, your experience of true life will grow too.

Giving your life to Jesus is a lot like arriving on an island paradise. You've made it, but it would be silly to stay at the airport. You've got the rest of your life (and all eternity!) to explore the sights, smells, and sounds of the kingdom God has opened up to you. You don't have to earn it, it's just handed to you. A gift!

Where should you start? Jesus commanded his followers to "Make disciples... baptizing them... and teaching them to obey everything I have commanded you" (Matthew 28:18-20). Baptism is a symbol of what Jesus has done for you and your faith in him. You've become a disciple of Jesus and the obeying part will take a lifetime, so getting baptized is your next step. If Jesus commands it, then we do it, right? And so should you.

In Manifest Church we baptize people by dunking them under the water, as practiced in the New Testament. When you go under, this symbolizes you dying to your old self and your sin. When you're raised up, this symbolizes your 'resurrection' into a new life with Jesus. Getting baptized is a public, tangible way to show God and the world that Jesus is now your Life.

Your guidebook for your new life, as you've probably guessed, is the Bible. Could you try to explore the island without the guidebook? Sure, but you're going to miss all kinds of things you'd never know about without it.

Your new life has four 'zones' to explore: Your union with God, the love of God, your identity in God, and the power of God. "Your life is hidden with Christ in God," (Colossians 3:3) so exploring your new life means exploring God himself. God is the final and eternal frontier.

You can explore:

Your union with God. You have been united with God the Father. Explore that relationship! Dive into worship, prayer, listening to his voice, and studying your Bible. Manifest Mornings will too!

The love of God. You've been given grace and mercy to forgive all your failures. You're totally loved and accepted as family. These aren't just words; they're experiences God wants you to embrace, journeys you can take as you learn to accept them by faith.

Your identity in God. What does it mean to be God's child? To be an embodiment of his love, light, and truth? Who you believe you are profoundly shapes your life. Let God define that for you!

The power of God. God's Spirit, now living in you, gives you power to be who he calls you to be. What does it mean to depend on him? How do we access this power? How do we share it with people who need a touch from God? Explore that!

Jesus says God's life—his kingdom—is like a little bit of yeast that multiplies and takes over a ball of dough, raising it into something bigger and more delicious than it was before (Matthew 13:33). Let Jesus be your life. Let him into every part of your thinking, feeling, and choosing so he can change you and make your life a gift to the world around him.

You're not alone! You're here with fellow Believers with wisdom to tap into. You also know unsaved people who think of Christianity as "do's and don'ts." You can be their tour guide as they consider faith in Christ for themselves. Share your experiences with them! They might just say, "You know what, that sounds like a wonderful place. I'll have to check that out."

NOW... RESPOND

First, talk to God about which of the four 'zones' you want to explore.

Second, it's time to obey Jesus and get baptized! We'll have a hot tub ready for baptisms on Manifest Mornings once a month or so, complete with a change of clothes and towels for you to use. You can come forward when the invitation is given one of those mornings or let us know ahead of time. All you'll need to do is answer a simple question with a yes: **Is Jesus Christ your Master and only Saviour?** In other words, you'll publicly declare your faith in Christ as we help you take this exciting step.

DAY THIRTEEN

How Should I Pray?

It's been almost two weeks since you began this book. Now is probably a good idea to pause and take some time to explore what prayer is, why it's important, and cover some basic principles. Sound good?

Prayer... is talking to God. There isn't any official vocabulary you're supposed to use, and you definitely don't have to try to sound "holy" or "christian" or anything else.

Jesus said, "When you pray, say, "Father..." In other words, when you pray, think of it like you're a child approaching their dad to talk. Your Father in heaven is the perfect Dad, so treat him that way. Praying to "God" is technically okay, but God is such a vague idea. "Dad" is much more personal, which is important, because your connection to him is your lifeline:

- He truly wants to hear what you're thinking and feeling, even if he knows what you're going to say—and even if he's heard it a million times.
- He doesn't want you to pretend you're someone you're not, so keep it real and raw.
- He'd rather you tell him how mad you are at him than give him the silent treatment.
- He loves to take care of you, so let him know what you need.
- He loves to give good gifts, so ask him for his richest blessings!
- He will forgive you no matter what you've done.
- If you haven't spoken to him for awhile, he won't hold it against you. He just wants to re-connect!
- Even if you don't know how to express what you're feeling, he wants you to try.
- If you don't have anything to say, that's fine. He loves just hanging out with you because he thinks you're amazing.
- Don't just ask for stuff. Tell him how amazing he is, what you're thankful for, etc.

You're going to need to form two important prayer habits as you grow up in your faith, and they go hand in hand. First of all, you're going to need to learn to pray out loud. Secondly, you're going to have to learn to pray out loud *with other Believers.*

Praying out loud is powerful. There's something profound about hearing yourself say things. Feelings and ideas are abstract, and they have a way of swirling around like dry leaves in our brain until we put words to them. Hearing yourself pray can help your faith seem more real to you. And praying with others—out loud—is really important. In the book of Acts, the first Christians started getting persecuted for their faith. Luke records that,

> "...They raised their voices together in prayer to God... After they prayed, the place where they were meeting was shaken. And they were all filled with the Holy Spirit and spoke the word of God boldly." (Acts 4:24,31)

When you pray out loud with other Believers, you'll realize you aren't alone in your struggles. You'll hear people praying about the same sorts of things that are on your mind. This will encourage you and infuse you with fresh boldness to live for Jesus.

> You're going to have to learn to pray out loud *with other Believers.*

Sure, you might feel like you're not as "good at it" as other people are—or that your prayers feel lame or silly. But God loves it when his children come together as a family to face the world. And believe me, the long-time Believers will find your "less refined" prayers refreshing and they'll want to recapture that for themselves.

NOW... RESPOND

I want you to block off fifteen minutes to spend with God in prayer today or tomorrow. Yes, fifteen. Yes, you'll run out of formal things to say. That's okay. Tell him that. Just go with it for the whole fifteen minutes. You'll end up saying what's really on your mind.

Secondly, I want you to find another Believer to pray out loud with this week. Or maybe pray out loud during your prayer time at Life Group. Press through your shyness and just do it! You'll be glad you did.

DAY FOURTEEN

Prayer That Changes Things

Yesterday you learned some 'prayer basics' that will help you grow a strong lifeline to your Father in heaven. That life-line through Jesus is the channel he uses to change the world. Jesus puts it this way:

"I am the vine; you are the branches. If you remain in me and I in you, you will bear much fruit; apart from me you can do nothing. If you do not remain in me, you are like a branch that is thrown away and withers; such branches are picked up, thrown into the fire and burned. If you remain in me and my words remain in you, ask whatever you wish, and it will be done for you. This is to my Father's glory, that you bear much fruit, showing yourselves to be my disciples" (John 15:5-8).

In other words, *you're connected to Jesus, the Source of all life and change in the world; so live like it.*

If you don't live in light of this connection, he says, you won't reap the benefits. But if you depend on this connection with Jesus for life and power, and live like the metaphor is physically true, God sends his life through you to change the world.

This is awesome! Think of the imagery: Jesus, the Vine, is seated at the right hand of God in heaven, invisible to our eyes. But we are connected to him, located on earth, visible to everyone. And the fruit is visible, too.

Which means—and you really need to grasp this—*you and I are the place where the invisible becomes visible*, where the resources of heaven meet the needs of earth, where the prayer "Your kingdom come, your will be done, on earth as it is in heaven" becomes a tangible reality. We are the real estate where the spiritual current of God's love takes on flesh, where it becomes a hug, a gift, an encouraging word, a sacrifice, or maybe even a full-on miracle.

But it all begins with prayer: "If you remain in me and my words remain in you, ask whatever you wish, and it will be done for you." In other words, Jesus is saying, "As you let me fill you with my love and power, your imagination will be captured by who I am and what I can do. You'll begin asking for things that I want too, and I'll do them... through you."

When we pray in sync with God's will, little bits of heaven manifest on earth as God answers our prayers. All of heaven is poised to flow towards earth, but God waits for people willing to give themselves to this grand mission. When the branch asks the Vine, "Could you please send some more sap so I can bear more fruit?" the Vine never says, "More fruit? We don't do that sort of thing." No, the branch is asking the Vine for something perfectly consistent with what the Vine is and what it wants to do.

When we pray, we often use words like, "In Jesus' name, Father, please do such-and-such." The actual name of Jesus is powerful, but his name also refers to his character, his authority, his power, his will.

You're connected to Jesus... live like it.

If I were an ambassador for my country, when I spoke I would be authorized to speak for Canada, in sync with our foreign policies and values wherever I traveled abroad. In the same way, I'm called to live and pray "in the name of Jesus," representing him in everything I say, pray and do.

NOW... RESPOND

When you pray, you're a child approaching your loving Father. But you're also a branch on the Vine of Christ, asking him to do what he loves to do: Make the invisible visible. So pray 'in the name of Jesus,' and while you're at it, pray for a few people in your world that don't know him yet. Ask God to reveal the truth of Jesus to them, to manifest his love for them. You can know beyond a shadow of a doubt you're praying according to his will—and you can probably count on becoming part of the answer somehow.

DAY FIFTEEN
Worship and Praise

As I've said before in this book, your new life in Christ is all about responding to who God is and what he's done for you through Jesus.

- Jesus' perfect life shows us that God is holy and perfect.
- Jesus' death for our sins shows us that God is love.
- Jesus' resurrection shows us God is all-powerful.
- Jesus' sending his Spirit sent be with us and within us shows us that God is ever-present and the Source of all life.
- Jesus' promise to return to restore all things and usher in a heavenly paradise forever shows us God is eternal.

God is so amazing that if we grasp who he truly is, we'll be left in perpetual awe that we even get to know him, let alone be one of his children. What Jesus did for us is so amazing that if we even begin to grasp the wonder of his gifts we'll be blown away and left in perpetual gratitude.

It's no exaggeration, then, to say that in many ways your new life in Christ is all about thanking, praising, and worshipping God, above all else and from now on.

To Paul, the only logical response to who God is and what he's done is this: "Therefore, I urge you, brothers and sisters, in view of God's mercy, to offer your bodies as a living sacrifice, holy and pleasing to God—this is your true and proper worship" (Romans 12:1). Your life becomes one big grateful sacrifice to the loving God who spared no expense—not even the death of his own Son—to grant you the life you were born to live.

Here on earth, "we see only a reflection as in a mirror," Paul says. We've only begun to grasp the reality we've waded into. But when we get to heaven, he says, "then we shall see face to face. Now I know in part; then I shall know fully, even as I am fully known." (I Corinthians 12:13). Can you even imagine?

A day is coming when we'll join "a great multitude" in heaven, worshipping God "like the roar of rushing waters and like loud peals of thunder, shouting: "Hallelujah! For our Lord God Almighty reigns. Let us rejoice and be glad and give him glory!" (Revelation 19:7).

Even the beings who live in the presence of God before his throne through all eternity worship him:

> "Whenever the living creatures give glory, honour and thanks to him who sits on the throne and who lives for ever and ever, (they) fall down before him who sits on the throne and worship him who lives for ever and ever. They lay their crowns before the throne and say: "You are worthy, our Lord and God, to receive glory and honour and power for you created all things, and by your will they were created and have their being." (Revelation 4:9-11).

We worship and praise God because he's worthy of every honour we can give him. Those heavenly beings would tell you that spending your life on Jesus is worth it because this life is a dress rehearsal for heaven. Remember? We live and pray that in everything, "Your kingdom come, your will be done, on earth as it is in heaven."

So we tell him how amazing he is. We worship him expressively— clapping, bowing down, lifting our hands to show him we're depending on him. We sing to him (both by ourselves and together) about how great he is. (This is why we sing in church, by the way).

You might be thinking, "Singing isn't really my thing." But it's *God's thing*, and he loves it when we honour him in that way. Or maybe you're thinking, "Bowing down to God feels weird." That's because we're not used to giving someone else that much honour. But again, God is worthy of your worship. It's how we show him (not just tell him), "You're God, and I'm not."

NOW... RESPOND

On your own: Read Psalm 150 out loud as a "worship prayer" to God. Notice how expressive it is! During Manifest Mornings on Sunday, sing the songs as worship to God. Imagine him sitting on his heavenly throne in front of you, as if you're worshipping him with that multitude of Believers. Let loose and express your praise with your body. Have fun with the music. You'll be surprised by how refreshing it is!

DAY SIXTEEN
An Introduction to the Bible

You can probably tell by now that the Bible is really important for your life as a Believer. I've been quoting it all over the place, unpacking and applying it to every topic we've discussed so far. What I'd like to do today is explain why it's so important and what it's for, so you can make the most of studying it for yourself.   First of all, let's define a few terms.

Technically speaking, the Bible isn't just a book; it's a collection of books—sixty six, to be exact—thirty nine of them belonging to a cluster of books we call the *Old Testament*, and twenty-seven of them found in what we call the *New Testament*.

The two "Testaments" refer to two covenants God made with mankind. A covenant is "an agreement that brings about a relationship of commitment between God and his people."

The first covenant "agreement" between God and humanity—running through the *Old* Testament—was based on keeping the Jewish law so they could enjoy his blessing. It was grounded most specifically in the ten commandments.

The books found in the Old Testament trace the creation of the universe, the "fall" of humans into sin, God giving them his laws to guide their lives towards a better world, and their utter failure to live up to that law. During this era, God called a man named Abraham to be his friend— and the founding member of a new nation that was supposed to belong to God and share his light with the world. Abraham's descendants would become known as the Hebrew people (modern day Jews), and would eventually form the nation we now call Israel. The books that unpack this era are generally referred to as 'the Law.'

Along the way, God also raised up prophets to foretell the coming of a Messiah figure who would rescue his people from their sins and inaugurate a new era of God's kingdom on earth based on a "new" covenant (testament). The books the prophets wrote are simply referred to as 'the Prophets.' All of the Bible is considered "scripture."

In a very real sense, the larger story running through the entire Bible points to the coming of this Messiah. The books found in the New Testament pick up the story during a dark slice of Israel's history when the Jewish nation had been usurped by the Roman Empire and was living under Roman domination. Enter Jesus Christ, the promised Messiah. The entire New Testament unpacks the details of Christ's life and the arrival of his new covenant in the books of Matthew, Mark, Luke, and John, which we call the "Gospels."

One book (called Acts) explains how the Church began right after Jesus' death and resurrection. The rest of the New Testament is devoted to showing us how we're supposed to live in light of what Christ accomplished. These books are called the *Epistles*, which are letters written by Christ's first disciples to help the fledging Churches grow in their faith. The book of Revelation unveils God's plan for the end of earth as we know it and how eternity will unfold from there on.

So... other than the obvious reasons, like the history lesson I just shared with you, why do we make such a big deal about the Bible?

First of all, because Jesus did. He quoted it all the time during his lifetime, showing us that it was his ultimate reference point for truth and life and everything in between. On one occasion he said,

> "Do not think that I have come to abolish the Law or the Prophets; I have not come to abolish them but to fulfill them. For truly I tell you, until heaven and earth disappear, not the smallest letter, not the least stroke of a pen, will by any means disappear from the Law until everything is accomplished. Therefore anyone who sets aside one of the least of these commands and teaches others accordingly will be called least in the kingdom of heaven, but whoever practices and teaches these commands will be called great in the kingdom of heaven" (Matthew 5:17-19).

The second reason the Bible is such a big deal is because, as the Apostle Paul reminds us, "All Scripture is God-breathed and is useful for teaching, rebuking, correcting and training in righteousness, so that the servant of God may be thoroughly equipped for every good work." (II Timothy 3:16,17).

Because God inspired scripture, the Bible is quite literally God's written word. And "the word of God," we're told, "is alive and active. Sharper than any double-edged sword, it penetrates even to dividing soul and spirit, joints and marrow; it judges the thoughts and attitudes of the heart" (Hebrews 4:12).

Why do we make such a big deal about the Bible? First of all, because Jesus did.

Through his word, God guides us, challenging our thinking, our life choices, and even our motives. As we respond to his word, our lives change.

But the most important thing the Bible does for us is explain how to put our faith in Jesus so we can experience him personally. The religious people of his day had a tough time grasping that. Jesus said, "These are the very Scriptures that testify about me, yet you refuse to come to me to have life" (John 5:40). Hearing God through the Bible is so important that Jesus declared, "People shall not live by bread alone, but by every word that comes from the mouth of God" (Matthew 4:4).

God speaks his word all kinds of ways, but the most reliable way is through the Bible. This "written word" gives us an unchanging standard to live by, a pattern to discern the truth by, and an example to compare our lives to. Without it, we tend to make up our lives as we go and end up missing what God has for us.

NOW... RESPOND

If you don't have a Bible yet, snag a free one from the Welcome Centre on Sunday or download YouVersion a free Bible app you can get in the App Stores.

The Bible is a big, thick, intimidating book to start reading. I get that. What's different about the Bible is that the Author, God himself, promises to guide us with his Spirit as we learn to study it for ourselves.

So maybe start there. Tell God you're not sure where to start, and that you need his help to begin. Tomorrow I'm going to show you how to get started!

DAY SEVENTEEN

How to Study the Bible: Look

Today you're going to start learning how to study the Bible for yourself.

The most important thing you can bring to Bible Study is the right attitude: That the Bible is God's Word, meaning you are expecting God to communicate with you through what you read. As you read yesterday, you're expecting to connect with Jesus and walk away changed in some way. In many ways, it's not what you "get out of it" that matters as much as what God gets out of you.

The Bible is a primary tool for making you into the disciple you're meant to be, so you should read and study it regularly. Knowing God is going to speak to you through the Bible means you're not just studying books like you did in school; think of it more like a conversation with God. Ask him to open his Word to you, to help you see and hear what he wants you to. Jesus promised us, promised you, "When he, the Spirit of Truth comes, he will guide you into all truth." (John 16:13). So talk to him throughout the process!

You're probably wondering, how does Bible Study *work?* Well, James (Jesus' brother) tells us in plain English how to get started:

"Do not merely listen to the word, and so deceive yourselves. Do what it says. Anyone who listens to the word but does not do what it says is like a man who looks at his face in a mirror and, after looking at himself, goes away and immediately forgets what he looks like. But the man who looks intently into the perfect law that gives freedom, and continues to do this, not forgetting what he has heard, but doing it - he will be blessed in what he does" (James 1:22-25).

In this short passage, you'll notice variations of three verbs in this paragraph: *Look, listen*, and *do*. This tells you how you're supposed to handle what you read. So take his advice.

First of all, when you study the Bible, *look*—and look *intently*. Drill down and focus. Don't just read it once! I often read a section over once, then twice, maybe even reading it out loud, since that's how the early Believers would have heard it.

But intently also means "with intent." So what's your intent? What do you hope to get out of it? According to James, our intent should be some version of "to hear what God says, and to put it into practice." In other words, if you're just reading recreationally, don't expect to get much out of it. If you're reading on the lookout for things that could change your life, God will reveal them to you.

What do you look for? To begin with, for words or phrases that stand out to you. Generally speaking, ask yourself, "What is the author actually saying?"

As you know from reading other books and conversations with people on an every day basis, sometimes what is *said* is different than what is *meant*. Metaphors generally shouldn't be taken literally, for example. Some books are poetry and more figurative; some are history; and some are more teaching oriented.

"When he, the Spirit of Truth comes, he will guide you into all truth." (John 16:13). So talk to him throughout the process!

Also be aware that in each of the books of the Bible, there is a certain flow to the writing. As you read, larger ideas are being developed. That little nugget of truth you noticed is a part of that bigger idea. We call this *context*. Understanding the wider context will help you understand the smaller nuggets more accurately and easily.

Here are a few questions to help you see what God wants you to see as you look intently into his Word.

Is there:

- A command to obey?
- Something you should stop doing?
- Something you should start doing?
- Something to praise or thank God for?
- Something new you didn't know before?
- Something you know but you've been forgetting?
- A sin you should confess to God?
- A lesson you need to learn?
- An idea you don't understand?
- An image or metaphor that helps you grasp a concept?
- A situation you resonate with?
- Something you need to pray about?
- A concept that sheds light on a problem or issue you're facing?
- An idea that reminds you of something else you read in the Bible?

How long do you look? Well, you don't have to see all of these things in everything you read. One or two would be nice! But as James says, don't stop looking until you see yourself—your life, or your situation—in the mirror. In other words, God wants to show you something that reminds you... of you. It could be a problem similar to yours, a struggle you have in common, an idea you've been pondering, something you need, something you like, etc. You get the idea. The key to an exciting Bible is seeing yourself in the mirror and bringing that to Jesus.

NOW... RESPOND

Today, practice on these two verses:

"If any of you lacks wisdom, you should ask God, who gives generously to all without finding fault, and it will be given to you. But when you ask, you must believe and not doubt, because the one who doubts is like a wave of the sea, blown and tossed by the wind" (James 1:6,7)

Start by asking the Holy Spirit to help you see what you need to see, then *look intently*. What stands out to you, and why? Use the bullet point questions to get you started. And remember to pray about what you learn!

DAY EIGHTEEN
How to Study the Bible: Listen and Do

Yesterday you got the first part of a crash course on how to study the Bible. To refresh your memory, we drew our guidelines from this passage, written by James, the brother of Jesus:

"*Do* not merely *listen* to the word, and so deceive yourselves. *Do* what it says. Anyone who *listens* to the word but does not *do* what it says is like a man who *looks* at his face in a mirror and, after *looking* at himself, goes away and immediately forgets what he *looks* like. But the man who *looks* intently into the perfect law that gives freedom, and continues to do this, not forgetting what he has *heard*, but *doing* it - he will be blessed in what he *does*" (James 1:22-25).

James uses variations of three action words over and over again: *Look, listen,* and *do.* Yesterday we unpacked what it means to *look*—to study God's word *intently*, looking for something that connects with our lives, kind of like like seeing ourselves in the mirror. Today we're going to dive into *listening* and *doing.* I'm putting those two together because they overlap in very practical ways.

When you've seen something that piques your interest or applies to your life in the Bible verses you're studying, assume God is the One who pointed it out. In other words, consider it God's initiative, which means the ball is in your court to respond. Ask the Holy Spirit to show you what else he wants you to know about what you're reading. Ask him how he wants you to put it into practice. Then *listen* for his wisdom and it will come.

When you study the scriptures with God's guidance, something amazing happens: What God *said* to people *in general* becomes what God is *saying* to you *personally, today.*

Let's say you've read something like, "Love your enemies" and it stands out immediately, because you're thinking of someone who's been a royal pain in the butt lately. Ask God, "Okay, I get it. Bob is like my enemy and I'm supposed to love him. But how? Please show me."

When the who, what, where, and when becomes clear, it's time to move to the next step—to do what you're supposed to do. When you've seen something God is highlighting for you and listened for his guidance, it's time ask him for power to obey what you've read. In this case it might be to forgive Bob, or maybe to ask his forgiveness for your bad attitude towards him.

That's where the real blessing (benefit) in Bible Study comes, James says: Not in the reading, not in the looking, not in the listening (even though that's really important), but in the *doing*. It's in the doing that we see the power of God's word really come alive in us and around us.

There's more to Bible study than this, obviously—but everything else is built on this simple progression: *Look, listen, and do.*

In your Life Group the same principles apply to Bible Study as a group, with the added bonus that other eyes are looking into the Word, other ears are listening for God's guidance, and other people are wrestling with how to put it into practice like you are. Studying the Bible with other Believers is a great way to learn how to do it more effectively.

NOW... RESPOND

If you don't have a Bible yet, snag a free copy from the Welcome Centre on Sunday or download the free YouVersion Bible App from the App Stores.

But now it's your turn!

Find the book of Mark in your Bible, in the New Testament. Start with Chapter One, and study verses 1-13 using the guidelines I shared with you in this chapter. Don't worry about what you don't understand yet, and focus on what grabs you instead. *Go!*

If you have questions or get stuck, just find a fellow Believer you know and see if they can help you understand what you're reading.

I find it helpful to write things down. Write down what you notice as you look. Write down what you think God might be saying to you about it as you listen. And write down what you think you're supposed to do with it. It might feel awkward at first, but don't worry, you'll learn!

DAY NINETEEN

Confessing Your Sins

The human heart was created to thrive. You were designed to enjoy life, laughter, peace, love, adventure, and inspiration. When sin entered the world, death oozed into all of creation along with it, touching everything and everyone.

Now we all fall short of our potential (never mind falling short of God's perfection). We all sin, screw up, break things, ruin relationships, lie to cover our tracks, hurt people (both on purpose and by accident), and do it over and over again.

When we screw up, we feel guilty, and we *should*—in the same way touching a hot stove should burn our finger. But there's a world of difference between guilt and condemnation. Guilt is a consequence; condemnation is a verdict. Guilt is designed to move us toward restoration; condemnation is designed to weigh us down with shame.

Paul wrote, "There is now no condemnation for those who are in Christ Jesus" (Romans 8:1). None. That's because on the cross, Jesus bore our condemnation and shame for us. Now the Father can pour out his love on us instead of punishment.

This doesn't mean you should never feel *guilty*. You should feel guilt (sadness, grief, and regret) for hurting yourself and others, including the Father who paid so much to bring you into his family. Guilt helps us own up to our failures so we can do better next time.

That said, God doesn't want us to *stay* guilty. Even though you never need to feel ashamed again, you most certainly will—but the problem will be on your end, not God's. When we do something particularly bad, it's hard to believe what Jesus did for us can cover *that*. But it does!

This is why God wants us to confess our sins to him and to others, especially the ones we've hurt. It brings hidden things into the light so they can be dealt with. It paves the way for grace to flow so we can put our grievances behind us permanently and feel forgiven. John wrote these powerful words:

"If we walk in the light, as he is in the light, we have fellowship with one another, and the blood of Jesus, his Son, purifies us from all sin. If we claim to be without sin, we deceive ourselves and the truth is not in us.If we confess our sins, he is faithful and just and will forgive us our sins and purify us from all unrighteousness" (I John 1:7-9).

To confess means owning up to something by putting it into words. It means agreeing with God and admitting that you've screwed up and sinned, guilty as charged.

Confessing our sins, both to God and each other, means walking out of the darkness of guilt into the light of God's grace. It brings our junk into the open so his love can touch and change us. God's grace is the foundation for true fellowship with each other because no one is perfect. We all need the same Saviour.

To forgive means to cleanse, to wipe clean, and—my favourite is this one—"to pick up and carry away." God doesn't just forgive you; he wants you to experience the freedom of that forgiveness by feeling it emotionally. He wants to pick up your guilt and shame—the self-condemnation that's been weighing on you—so he can lift it from your shoulders and carry it away forever. As Psalm 103:12 says, "As far as the east is from the west, so far has he removed our transgressions from us." Wow! Time to put this into practice.

NOW... RESPOND

Take a few minutes to study I John 1:5-10 using the *look, listen, do* framework you learned about this past week.

When you're done, ask the Holy Spirit to shine his light on your heart and help you see the sins and failures he wants you to confess. When you think of something, God has brought it to mind, so agree with him. Say, "Father, I agree. When I _____, that was sin, and I'm sorry."

Now tell him how committing that sin makes you feel—guilty, ashamed, maybe embarrassed. Let yourself feel it.

Finally, tell him you don't want to carry those emotions anymore and ask him to come lift them from you forever. Imagine him coming and doing it, and thank him for his forgiveness.

DAY TWENTY
Forgiving Others

People hurt people. People disappoint us, wound us, frustrate us, let us down, stab us in the back, humiliate us, reject us, betray us, hurt our feelings, and neglect us. And those are just our friends!

When we're hurt, we experience negative emotions—and the deeper the wound, the more intensely those emotions grip us. But like I pointed out yesterday, your heart isn't designed to carry bitterness, anger, rage, unforgiveness, and frustration. Negative emotions eat us alive, and the longer we hold onto them the more damage they inflict on our souls.

You need to forgive people who hurt you—even when it's hard! As someone has said, "Refusing to forgive is like drinking poison and expecting the other person to die." Forgiveness isn't just for the offender. It's God's ordained way to free *us* of bitterness so we can thrive again, rising above our pain despite what we've been through.

Forgiving someone doesn't mean ignoring the consequences of their actions; it means letting go of your anger and what that's doing to your own heart and trusting God to work on theirs. For example, a young woman can forgive her abusive boyfriend for the pain he's caused her and break up with him at the same time.

So… "Forgive one another if any of you has a grievance against someone," The Apostle Paul says, adding these important words: "Forgive as the Lord forgave you" (Colossians 3:13). This tells us a few amazing things about forgiveness.

First of all, forgiveness is a command to obey, not an option to consider. You could say that from now on, forgiveness is your way of life. We've been forgiven for everything we've ever done (or will do) at the price of Jesus' own life. How can we accept that forgiveness on one hand and refuse it to someone else on the other?

The person who offended us doesn't deserve forgiveness, but neither do we. Jesus' sacrifice for us—(guilty-as-charged rebels)—frees us to forgive others like we've been forgiven by God. So we forgive freely, graciously, and miraculously. Especially when people don't deserve it. We never look more like Jesus than when we forgive.

And it's not just for 'the big stuff.' Forgiveness even applies to our grievances—stuff that ticks us off or even just annoys us. It applies to anything, big or small, festering in our souls.

When God forgave you, there was an actual *exchange:* You offered him your sin, guilt and shame—and he traded it for his grace, pardon, and love.

When Paul says we're supposed to forgive others *like God forgave us,* the same thing applies. God wants you to experience the freedom of forgiving others in the form of *emotional release.* He wants to pick up the anger, bitterness and hate that's been weighing on you—so he can lift it from your shoulders and carry it away forever. And then he wants to replace that anger with grace, love, and peace. Sound good?

Time to show you how!

NOW... RESPOND

1. Take a few minutes to scan your heart for any lingering frustration with people.

2. Admit the anger is there instead of brushing it off with, "Yeah, but I've dealt with that. I'm good."

3. Tell God what the person did to you, in detail, including how this makes you feel. Let yourself feel the anger, the betrayal, the hurt, whatever it is.

4. Ask yourself: Do you want to carry that anger, bitterness, and hate, and let it fester in your soul? If not, tell God you forgive the person who hurt you.

5. Ask Jesus to lift those negative emotions off of you and take them away forever. Then ask him to fill you with his grace and love instead. Picture him lifting it all away and blessing you.

6. Now think back to what the person did for you. Do you feel emotionally free yet? If not, there may be something else to forgive.

7. Thank God for his grace in your life!

DAY TWENTY-ONE

Hearing God's Voice

Of all the questions I'm asked by Believers wanting to grow in their faith, the most common one is this: "How can I learn to hear God's voice?" I bet you're wondering about that, too.

In John Chapter ten, Jesus explained that we can learn a lot about listening to God by watching a shepherd relate to his sheep. "The sheep listen to his voice," Jesus points out. "He calls his own sheep by name and leads them… His sheep follow him because they know his voice" (John 10:3,4). In the same way, Jesus says, "My sheep listen to my voice. I know them, and they follow me" (John 10:27).

Listening to God is so important that when Jesus came to earth he said, "People shall not live by bread alone, but by every word that comes from the mouth of God" (Matthew 4:4).

Did you get that? Jesus' sheep hear his voice! Jesus is continuously speaking to every one of us, and hearing from him is like food. His word is the bread you need to eat and digest every single day. God has been speaking to you already, is speaking to you today, and will speak to you tomorrow. As God speaks, he'll guide you, reassure you, protect you, and help you love the people all around you.

One of the marks of a true Believer is that they take God's voice seriously Paul says, "Those that are led by the Spirit of God are the children of God" (Romans 8:14). "They follow me," Jesus says. And he calls each of us by name. The flock is led together, as one—but we follow because he speaks to us individually, personally, and intimately.

What does God's voice sound like? I hate to sound sarcastic, but God sounds a lot like… God. The best way to learn to recognize God's voice is to study the Bible. You've already learned that the Bible is the Word of God—in other words, it's the voice of God in writing. The Bible is a the perfect, authoritative record of who God is and what he says. And it's also (among other things) a book of stories about God speaking to people. As you study the Bible, you'll watch him speak to his followers, his angels, his creation, to his enemies, and even to people who don't believe he exists. As you get to know him and learn about how he has spoken, you'll learn to know his voice as naturally as any other voice in your life on a day-to-day basis. And God will never say anything that contradicts what he's already said in the Bible.

Jesus also says that his sheep, especially the ones who've been hanging around him, know his voice. Spending time with other sheep is a great way to hear his voice. In the sheep analogy, the sheep 'born yesterday' learn that when the guy with the staff calls, everybody gets up and moves. The next day when the guy speaks, it happens again. And again. Eventually the new sheep listens for herself, because she knows the voice of her Shepherd too.

Jesus wants everyone to become one of his sheep like you are. Once, surrounded by a crowd, Jesus "had compassion on them, because they were harassed and helpless, like sheep without a shepherd" (Matthew 9:36). "We all, like sheep, have gone astray," Isaiah wrote (Isaiah 53:6). This is why Jesus said, "I have other sheep that are not of this sheep pen. I must bring them also. They too will listen to my voice, and there will be one flock and one shepherd" (John 10:16).

God is speaking to everyone you meet, even though they don't usually recognize his voice. He's calling their name, drawing them to himself. It's an amazing gift to help someone tune into God's voice: "Hey, that's Jesus speaking to you. He loves you, and he wants you to come home!"

NOW... RESPOND

Take a few minutes to read John 10:1-27 on your own. Thank Jesus for being your shepherd, and ask him to help you listen to his voice. And then try something: Ask him a question. Ask, "Jesus, what would you like me to know about hearing your voice?" Quiet your heart, and see what comes to mind.

Knowing Jesus is speaking to people in your life, Believers or not, is such a relief. Look for evidence of God leading and speaking to people you know. When you see it, try pointing it out to them. People are usually really excited to know God has been talking to them!

DAY TWENTY-TWO
What to 'Listen' For

Yesterday I said God sounds… a lot like God. That probably left you thinking, "Yeah, but practically speaking, what does God's voice sound like?"

Jesus' sheep hear his "voice"—which means God "speaks"—but in the broadest sense, it's probably most accurate to say God *communicates*. This communication arrives in five different *forms* (verbal, visual, logical, intuitive, and physical), and it is delivered through three important *channels* (through his Spirit, other people, and our circumstances).

Verbal communication (using words) is the most obvious of the five forms. This includes God's written word, the Bible, but it also includes "every word that comes from the mouth of God," which, you'll remember, Jesus says we're supposed to live by (Matthew 4:4). Yes, God plants words or even sentences in our minds. I often have conversations with God—I speak (either in my head or out loud) then listen for his replies in my mind.

Visual communication is also common. When God speaks, his word often arrives in the form of images. Dreams, visions (which are like dreams while we're awake), pictures in our minds, or even things we see in the physical world can all be used by God to communicate with us. For example, as I pray, a picture of something often takes shape in my mind. Sometimes the picture is given by God to reveal something I need to know. The Holy Spirit often spoke to the prophets in the Old Testament this way.

God also packages his voice in the form of logic—in other words, by helping us grasp something really important. Once, when Jesus asked his disciples, "Who do you say that I am?" "Simon Peter answered, "You are the Messiah, the Son of the living God."Jesus replied, "Blessed are you, Simon son of Jonah, for this was not revealed to you by flesh and blood, but by my Father in heaven" (Matthew 16:16,17). Often, when God speaks through logic, we mistake our own thinking as the source instead of God. This is why Jesus had to point it out to Peter: "That was God speaking to you about that."

The fourth package is intuition. When God speaks intuitively, there are no words, no logical thought process to note, no pictures in our minds, we just *know* something all of a sudden. This happened to Jesus a lot. Quite often we read things like, "Jesus, knowing their thoughts, said…" I would say this is a fairly common package or form God's communication takes.

The fifth and final package God's communication takes is when God's communication takes physical form. We might feel a tingling sensation and a deep peace settle over us, or when God is healing someone it's not uncommon for them to feel a life-giving heat.

Sometimes I feel something like a hand lightly touching my head, and I know it's the Holy Spirit simply saying something like, "Hey, pay attention," or "You're on the right track." Sometimes God makes sure we feel physically loved, peaceful, safe, or convicted of our sin. It's important not to read too much into these physical packages, though. Think of them more like ripples a stone makes when thrown into a pond. The stone (God) is more important than the ripples.

There are two things you need to know about the five packages: One, they overlap a lot. So God might speak verbally as you're reading his word, and BAM—you suddenly just know you need to go talk to Bob, your neighbour about what happened yesterday. And then, BOOM—you feel a surge of joy as God says, "way to go!"

Secondly, while God can speak to you via all five forms, he probably has a favourite way to communicate with you. You may rarely get verbal and visual communication from God, because he most often speaks to you through intuition or logic, for example. Everyone is different! But now you know what to "listen for," so anything can happen from here on out. Tomorrow we'll talk about the three channels God most often uses to deliver these five packages.

NOW... RESPOND

For starters, you should probably re-read what you just read. Then take a few minutes to thank God that he speaks to you. Ask him to help you tune in to the ways he's been trying to get your attention. Then, ask him, "Lord Jesus, is there anything you'd like me to know right now?" Pay attention to any words, pictures, thoughts, intuitions, or physical cues he might be using to speak to you.

DAY TWENTY-THREE
God Speaks Through His Holy Spirit

The most direct way God speaks to us is by his Spirit.

Jesus says the Holy Spirit is our Counsellor. This is the same Holy Spirit Jesus depended on and listened to while he lived as a human on earth, showing us what's possible if we depend on him and listen to him like he did.

As you learned yesterday, the Holy Spirit packages his voice in the form of words. The most important words he'll speak are the ones already found in the Bible. He inspired the writers of the Bible to record what they did, so the Bible is God's voice on the page. When you read it, God is speaking to you. But the Spirit also speaks to us about other things. "As his anointing teaches you about all things and as that anointing is real, not counterfeit—just as it has taught you, remain in him" (I John 2:27).

The Holy Spirit also packages his voice visually. When the Spirit came upon people like tongues of fire after Jesus' resurrection, it was a fulfillment of a prophecy: "I will pour out my Spirit on all people. Your sons and daughters will prophesy, your young men will see visions, your old men will dream dreams" (Acts 2:17).

Jeremiah, an Old Testament prophet, wrote, "The word of the Lord came to me: "What do you see, Jeremiah?" "I see the branch of an almond tree," I replied." (Jeremiah 1:11). In other words, the "word" came as a picture in his mind, or a "vision."

The Holy Spirit also packages his voice in the form of our logic and thinking patterns. This is why Jesus said, "When He, the Spirit of truth comes, he will lead you into all truth" (John 16:13). In other words, sometimes he doesn't drop the truth in our laps. Sometimes, he leads us there as our minds progressively wrestle with and grasp what he's saying over time.

Fourthly, the Holy Spirit packages his voice in the form of our intuition, or a kind of "faith knowing." For example, Paul says, "the Spirit himself testifies with our spirit that we are God's children" (Romans 8:16). He's saying something to the effect of, "The Holy Spirit will help you *know* you belong to God. It will resonate deep within you." Sometimes people talk about these intuitive leadings of the Spirit "nudges" from God. In other words, we might get a feeling we ought to say or do something without totally understanding how or why. As we listen to those nudges and go with them, we often see in hindsight that the Holy Spirit was behind them.

Lastly, the Holy Spirit sometimes packages his voice in physical form. In Psalm twenty-nine, the writer was apparently watching a lightning storm and it prompted him to write, "The voice of the Lord is powerful; the voice of the Lord is majestic. The voice of the Lord breaks the cedars" (Psalm 29:4,5).

Other times, as I mentioned, the Holy Spirit might give us some kind of bodily cue that he's with us, that we're did something wrong (like maybe the heaviness of guilt), or that we're not supposed to do something (an "off" feeling) or a churning gut.

The main thing is to realize God has given us his Spirit to manifest the heart, love, power, and voice of Jesus to us here on earth. He lives within you and wants to communicate verbally, visually, logically, intuitively, and even physically with you.

One of the best ways to "practice" hearing from God is to ask him to show you how to love people. Then run with what he communicates. The worst case scenario is, you tried to do something nice for someone.

NOW... RESPOND

Thank God that he's given his Spirit to be with you and in you. Thank him for speaking to you. Ask him to speak to you and guide you throughout every day—then listen for the verbal, visual, logical, intuitive, and physical messages he'll initiate.

Don't just wait for him to speak; speak to him! Ask him questions, then "listen" for an answer. Ask for wisdom, then accept his guidance. In whatever situation you find yourself, get in the habit of asking, "What would you like me to know right now?" Train yourself to listen for his reply.

DAY TWENTY-FOUR
God Speaks Through People

The past few days you've been learning about how God speaks to you. You've learned about the five packages his voice takes as he communicates with us—verbal, visual, logical, intuitive, and physical. Yesterday, you learned God often delivers these messages directly by his Spirit. If you feel God has been using this book to help you grow in your faith, you already know what you're going to learn about today: *God speaks through people.*

First, *God speaks through people verbally.* He inspired people like Paul, Peter, John, and King David to write books within the larger Bible. He also gives prophets messages to share with people. But he also uses regular people all around you to deliver messages all the time. Often they don't even realize God has been using them!

God uses parents to speak to children. He uses preachers to talk to churches every Sunday. He uses books, conversations, and all kinds of other means to deliver messages to his people. These messages will help you see God more clearly, help you see yourself more clearly, or help you see your path in life more clearly.

Second, *God speaks through people visually.* He gets our attention through art, movies, TV shows, billboards, and imagery people use in telling their own stories. I can't count how many times I've been watching a movie and a particular scene triggers something in my heart as I realize I've just seen a beautiful illustration of something God has been trying to teach me.

Third, God speaks through people logically. When you share what you're going through with a trusted friend or even a counsellor, they might help you think through what's going on, poke holes in your own logic that you needed to rework, or give you insight you couldn't have arrived at on your own.

Fourth, God speaks through people intuitively. Sometimes just hanging out with someone and watching how they handle situations helps the truth 'click.' There weren't any words, no logical thought process, just a dawning of comprehension somehow. God used a friend of mine to re-ignite my faith, in particular with praying for sick people to get well. It wasn't what he said; it was what he did. I think this is because, as the maxim goes, many things can't be taught; they can only be caught.

Fifth, God communicates with us through people physically. How many times have you received a hug just when you needed it? Just this week a friend left some candy at our place for me to enjoy, and I know it's a gift from them, but also from God. Or God might communicate his care and provision by sending you people to help you move into your new house, finish a yard project, or to babysit your children when you need a night out with your spouse.

Most times, God will use people to confirm what he's already starting to communicate with you in other ways. If something someone says seems to come right out of the blue, pray about it and ask God to show you if and how it's true. If it resonates with your heart and lines up with what the Bible teaches, it's probably from God. The prophet Isaiah understood all the ways God communicates with us. He put it this way:

> "As the rain and the snow come down from heaven, and do not return to it without watering the earth and making it bud and flourish, so that it yields seed for the sower and bread for the eater, so is my word that goes out from my mouth: It will not return to me empty, but will accomplish what I desire and achieve the purpose for which I sent it" (Isaiah 55:10,11).

See how many forms God's word takes? And notice the delivery systems: From God directly (his Spirit), through people (sower, eater) and through circumstances (the field, the growing crop). Awesome!

Another powerful implication is that God wants to speak to others... through you. As you receive his communication verbally, visually, logically, intuitively, and physically, you can pass it on to others. And sometimes, God will speak through you without you even knowing it. In particular, he wants to use you to help people who aren't believers in Jesus wake up to trust and love him too.

NOW... RESPOND

Take a few minutes to ask God to show you how he's been trying to communicate with you through people. Reflect on what he's saying. If you need to, feel free to process what you think you're hearing with other believers, maybe in your Life Group.

DAY TWENTY-FIVE
God Speaks Through Circumstances

Throughout the Bible we can read stories and examples of God speaking through people's circumstances.

While God can say whatever he wants, when he wants, when he communicates through our circumstances, he tends to keep it simple. This is because circumstances can be so easily misinterpreted. With that in mind, when God speaks to you through what's going on in your life, the message tends to be one of five varieties:

- You're blowing it.
- This isn't going to end well.
- I'm here.
- I love you.
- You need me.

You're blowing it. God usually lets the "cause and effect" of our sinful choices run their course. While he tries to convict us of our sin by his Spirit or through people on the front end with a warning, sometimes we don't get the message until we face truth on the back end with the consequences. "Endure hardship as discipline," the writer to the Hebrews says. "God is treating you as his children...God disciplines us for our good, in order that we may share in his holiness" (Hebrews 12:7,10). You might say God is asking, "So... how's this working for you?"

This isn't going to end well. This one is like the "you're blowing it" message, but drawn out to it's logical conclusion. Many of us, when faced with the consequences of our actions, keep doing the sinful or hurtful thing anyway. It would be incredibly unloving of God to "get us off the hook" or waive the consequences. Instead, he lets the pain of our mistakes paint a picture of where our choices are leading us. What he's looking for us for us to confess our sin so he can forgive us and lead us down a different path (I John 1:9).

I'm here. I can't count how many times a complicated situation just kind of "worked out" for no reason at all. Is it coincidence? It might be, or it could be God letting us know he's there, that he's watching us, that he cares about us. What he's looking for, of course, is for us to respond. To pay attention, to tune in to anything else he might be trying to say.

I love you. God sending Jesus said, "I love you." God giving you a life to live says, "I love you." God bringing you friends says, "I love you." God providing for your needs says, "I love you." God blocking your path or closing a door to keep you from a poor decision is God saying, "I love you." When God heals you or performs a miracle in your life, he's saying, "I love you."

God is love (I John 4:8), and so everything he does says "I love you," even if what he does is painful for a season. Every day, look for ways he is saying, "I love you," because there isn't a day in your life when he isn't saying it somehow, somewhere, through someone.

You need me. Paul said he celebrated his weaknesses and struggles because they reminded him he needed the power of Jesus (II Corinthians 12:9,10). God will often let life get out of hand, allowing difficult circumstances that make us feel out of control or inadequate in our own strength. The message is, "Look to me. Only I can give you what you need to thrive through this."

Even Jesus said he could do nothing without his Father empowering him! We can't save ourselves, change ourselves, or thrive without God. We need Jesus, and the more that message saturates our souls, the more his power will rest on us. He turns our weakness into strength (II Corinthians 12:9,10).

NOW... RESPOND

Take a few minutes to ask God how he's been trying to communicate with you through your circumstances. Pray about all five messages: "Lord, where have you been trying to say, "You're blowing it?" Where have you been trying to say, "I love you?" etc. Talk to him about what he reveals to your heart.

Choose someone you know to share what God has been saying to you through your circumstances. Ask them what they think God might be trying to say through theirs.

This week, ask some people who aren't Believers in Jesus yet how things are going. Look for evidence of God's communication with them (especially the "you need me" or "I love you" motifs—and point it out: "I think God is trying to say something to you."

DAY TWENTY-SIX
Joining in The Mission

Jesus launched his public mission on earth by recruiting regular people to follow him. He called these people his disciples, which is what we'd call an 'apprentice' today. Just before Christ ascended into heaven, he delegated the follow through for his entire mission to the disciples he had just trained. He said,

> "All authority in heaven and earth has been given to me.
> Therefore go and make disciples of all nations, baptizing them in
> the name of the Father and of the Son and of the Holy Spirit,
> and teaching them to obey everything I have commanded you.
> And surely I am with you always, to the very end of the age." ~
> *Matthew 28:18-20*

The mission is to help people like you and me become apprentices (disciples) of Jesus, to immerse us in the life of God (Father, Son, and Holy Spirit), and then teach us to obey everything Jesus commanded—which includes living for his disciple-making mission.

Here's a reality check: The reason Christian churches still exist today is because people of every age have accepted that mission. The faith torch has been passed down from generation to generation, breaking into new territory, changing new families, pushing back new darkness, rescuing new lost people, building steam for more than two thousand years—and now the mission has been shared with you.

Some of Jesus' disciples are gifted to teach, preach, and lead on a larger scale. That said, all of us, regardless of age or spiritual maturity, should be helping other Believers grow in their faith. For example, every one of us are called to:

- "Love each another" (I Thessalonians 4:9)
- "Instruct one another," (Romans 15:14)
- "Encourage one another" (II Corinthians 13:11)
- "Serve one another" (Galatians 5:1
- "Submit to one another" (Ephesians 5:21)
- "Have equal concern for each other" (I Corinthians 12:25)

- "Carry each other's burdens" (Galatians 6:2)
- "Confess your sins to each other and pray for each other" (James 5:16)

I call this the 'one-another-each-other' approach to disciple-making. It's the mission of God for average Joes like you and me. None of us need to wait for a 'super mentor' to grow in our faith. We just need to connect with other average Believers, depend on the power and presence of God's Spirit, and learn as we go.

It was the same for Jesus' disciples. "Come, follow me," he said, "and I will make you fishers of people!" (Mark 1:17).

That's the same message and mission that's been passed down to you. Jesus shares three important ideas here:

- **Follow me...** Your faith is about living in (*Abiding* in) Jesus and in his body, the Church.

- **And I will make you...** Jesus transforms us into something good and new (this is about your emerging *Identity* in him).

- **Fishers of people.** This means accepting his good news *Mission* to help all people discover true life in Christ.

This is our "AIM Dna." (AIM stands for **A**biding, **I**dentity, and **M**ission). It's Dna because these four ideas are the building blocks of your new life in Christ. All three of these themes have been woven into this book, but the last part of the book will focus on Mission in particular. This is where things get really exciting!

NOW... RESPOND

Take a few minutes to reflect on Matthew 28:18-20, as printed above. Talk to God about it—about your fears, your questions—and then tell him you accept the mission and want his help living it out.

DAY TWENTY-SEVEN
You, The Witness

On the day Jesus ascended into heaven, he wanted to make sure his disciples were crystal clear about their role in expanding his kingdom from then on. So he said,

> "You will receive power when the Holy Spirit comes on you; and you will be my witnesses in Jerusalem, and in all Judea and Samaria, and to the ends of the earth" (Acts 1:8).

You will be my *witnesses.* In many ways, God is "on trial" in the hearts and minds of people as they decide what to do with him. So he calls his disciples to "take the stand" and be cross-examined by the curious. The job of a witness is simple: Report what you've seen, heard, and experienced. Tell the truth, the whole truth, and nothing but the truth. That's it.

The original disciples had obviously witnessed a lot more than we have —they saw Jesus in action day after day preaching to crowds, walking on water, healing the sick, feeding the hungry, and healing people. They also saw him die for their sins and then appear in the flesh, the resurrected King over life and death.

What have you seen, heard, and experienced? Maybe not much, in your mind—but if you've put your faith in him, you've witnessed plenty:

- You've experienced his forgiveness
- You've experienced his love and acceptance
- You've been given a new start and a new identity in him
- You've been given a new spiritual family to belong to
- You're starting to experience him speaking to yo and guiding you throughout life
- Your heart is changing, and with it, some of your habits, desires, goals, and behaviour

So your mission is the same as theirs: To take the stand in life and share what you have seen, heard, and experienced when people need your testimony. Paul puts it this way: "Always be prepared to give an answer to everyone who asks you to give the reason for the hope that you have. But do this with gentleness and respect..." (I Peter 3:15).

Don't worry about what you *haven't* seen, heard, or lived. You don't have to know all the answers to all the questions or have all the key Bible verses memorized. You don't have to know all the big words Christians use (a lot of that churchy language should probably be dropped anyway).

Truthfully, you don't even have to have your life put together! Once, when Jesus cast some demons out of a naked homeless guy, he said, "Return home and tell how much God has done for you." So the man went away and told all over town how much Jesus had done for him" (Luke 8:39). Although, he did put clothes on first.

One time, a bunch of church people cornered a blind man Jesus had just healed and started peppering him with hard questions. I love his reply: "I don't know. One thing I do know. I was blind but now I see!" (John 9:25). He stuck to what he knew, and it was really hard to argue with an ex-blind guy.

That's what being a witness is all about. You may not know much, but Jesus has become real to you. He's saved you. And every week, you are witnessing more of who God is and what he's done for us, for you. You are a witness called to the witness stand to share your testimony—the truth, the whole truth, and nothing but the truth. That's totally worth talking about!

NOW... RESPOND

Remember, being Christ's witness begins with the Holy Spirit giving you power. That power will give you boldness to overcome your shyness and clarity when you open your mouth to speak. Begin your journey as a witness by taking two steps this week:

• Tell a Believer you know about something God has done for you
• Tell a friend who isn't a Believer yet something God has done for you.

DAY TWENTY-EIGHT
Boldness

After learning you are a witness for Jesus, part of you probably felt a twinge of anxiety in your gut. Or maybe a full-blown stomach ache.

We read Paul the Apostle say things like, "I am not ashamed of the gospel, because it's the power of God for salvation" (Romans 1:16). But then we often still find it hard to speak up and share our faith in Jesus when windows of opportunities present themselves.

Yesterday we learned that we shouldn't feel unqualified to be his witness, because all we have to do is share what we've seen, heard, and experienced—not what we haven't. But there are other reasons we might hesitate. We might be afraid of what people will think of us for believing in Jesus, or worried that we'll offend someone by sharing the truth when they're not ready to hear it. This is why the Believers in the book of Acts prayed for boldness in their witness: "Now, Lord, consider their threats and enable your servants to speak your word with great boldness" (Acts 4:29).

What is boldness? It's not just courage; it's using it. I like to say that boldness is what you get when you mix clarity with courage. God supplies the courage, and through his word, the Bible, we can find clarity to pair with it.

Why is clarity a prerequisite for boldness? Because it's not possible to feel confident about something we don't understand. One of the reasons we lack boldness in sharing our faith in Jesus is we don't understand it very well. So here's the good news, in a nutshell, for you to become familiar with. Jesus is the Son of God, (meaning, God himself). He:

1. Loved us so much that he became human and lived the perfect, sinless life we could never live—then gave us the credit for it so we could be approved and validated by God.

2. Died on the cross to pay for our sins and set us free from guilt and judgement, restoring our relationship with the Father (which is our core problem to begin with).

3. Rose from the dead to share his eternal life, victory and resurrection power with us—so we don't have to be in control or successful on our own strength.

4. Sent his Spirit to give us a new identity, a new faith family, a new mission, a new power, and a new union with God.

5. Will return for us one day so we can live and reign with him forever in a restored heaven and earth.

John says, "God loved the world so much that he gave his one and only Son, so that whoever believes in him won't perish but have eternal life" (John 3:16). Paul simplifies what Jesus did for us: "Christ died for our sins... was buried... (and) he was raised on the third day" (I Corinthians 15:3,4). He says in Romans 10:9,10, "If you confess with your mouth, "Jesus is Lord," and believe in your heart that God raised him from the dead, you will be saved.

NOW... RESPOND

First, ask God to give you boldness to speak his word and give you opportunities to do it.

Second, look over the gospel summary laid out above and ask God to show you who might need to hear parts of this message. Do you know anyone struggling with:

- Earning approval or validation, or living under disapproval?
- Guilt, shame, anger, bitterness, regret, disconnect from God?
- Control issues, feeling powerless, anxiety, workaholism?
- Identity, belonging, loneliness, aimlessness?
- Hopelessness, discouragement, despair?

These numbers correspond to the part of the gospel, listed above, that they may need most. Remember, when you speak up, you don't have to 'preach' at them; just share what you know as a fellow human on the road to meaning and a better life.

DAY TWENTY-NINE
The Work of The Holy Spirit

Yesterday you learned about growing boldness as you share Jesus with people who don't know him yet. Today's big lesson is, *it's not up to you.*

For one thing, the mission is ultimately God's. You've been learning all about that already. It's a huge relief knowing you don't have to invent a purpose for your life.

Secondly, God is already at work. Jesus said, "My father is always working, to this very day, and I too am working" (John 4:34). In other words, God invites us to join us in his work. He's already been trying to soften people's hearts to the truth. He's been drawing people to himself, arranging conversations and encounters with Believers, planting seeds of faith, growing discontent in their lives.

Most unsaved people haven't connected the dots yet, but the Holy Spirit has been at work in their hearts and minds. This means when you open your mouth to share your faith, you're not initiating a spiritual conversation, you're adding to it. As you listen to their stories, look for the evidence of God at work, and join him in the work in progress. Remember your own story: the day you finally put your faith in Christ was just one step in a journey that began long before that.

Things to look for: Honest questions about life and faith; places where something you're learning in your own life might be helpful for them too; struggles that make them question what life is really about; life changes that help put them in a more open headspace because that's what change does; and curiosity about what makes you tick.

Along the way, our job is simply to share the truth as plainly and honestly as we can. As Paul wrote, "How… can they (unbelievers) call on the one they have not believed in? And how can they believe in the one of whom they have not heard? And how can they hear without someone preaching to them? And how can anyone preach unless they are sent? As it is written: "How beautiful are the feet of those who bring good news!" (Romans 10:14,15).

We plant seeds of truth and water them through love and friendship, but God is the one who makes them sprout, grow, and bear fruit. God is the one who changes hearts and works miracles. It's not your job to transform someone's life, rescue them from sin, re-order their priorities, or make them give their lives to Jesus. The Holy Spirit is the one who convicts people of their sin (John 16:7-11),convinces them of their need for Jesus, and moves them to do something about it. And its up to them to respond with a yes or a no.

In all of this, God works through us. He invites us to partner with him. This is what we studied a few days ago; God works through you: "You will receive power when the Holy Spirit comes on you; and you will be my witnesses" (Acts 1:8). Jesus promises us that when the time comes to speak up, "do not worry about how you will defend yourselves or what you will say,for the Holy Spirit will teach you at that time what you should say" (Luke 12:11,12).

Understanding all this profoundly increases your boldness. The mission is God's. The message is God's. God is already at work in people's lives. It's his job to convince and save them. All you have to do, as John wrote, is to share "which we have heard, which we have seen with our eyes, which we have looked at and our hands have touched—this we proclaim concerning the Word of life" (I John 1:1).

When Jesus called his first disciples, they didn't fully understand who he was. They hadn't put their faith in him yet. They just hung out with him, took in what he said, and started putting it into practice. Somewhere along the line, they woke up and realized he was the Saviour of the world.

It's the same with unsaved people in your life: the seeds you're planting are helping them to start checking out Jesus—applying some of the things he said and did—before they fully believe it. At some point, they'll have to decide what they believe and clarify that with God.

NOW... RESPOND

Think of some spiritually lost people you know. Look for some of the signs I mentioned that might indicate God's work in people's lives. It's there; keep praying and looking until you find it, then pray for boldness to plant seeds of truth and love that prompt them to wrestle with who Jesus is and what he can do for them.

DAY THIRTY
Telling Your Story

All of this talk about being a witness of Jesus and for Jesus has probably got you thinking, *"Well, what have I seen? What have I heard? I'm new at this, so what have I experienced? What should I share? What should I leave out?"* Those are good questions. Let's take some time to start addressing them.

The first thing you need to settle is who the story about. Hint: It's not *you.* The purpose of sharing your faith isn't to draw people to yourself, it's to point to Jesus. So your real story isn't, "Well, I did this, then I did that, and then I realized the other thing, so I did this and that, and you should do it too." Not at all. Listen to how Paul describes how every one of us should tell our stories. It's a long quote, but worth every word:

> "As for you, you were dead in your transgressions and sins, in which you used to live when you followed the ways of this world and of the ruler of the kingdom of the air, the spirit who is now at work in those who are disobedient. All of us also lived among them at one time, gratifying the cravings of our flesh and following its desires and thoughts. Like the rest, we were by nature deserving of wrath.

> But because of his great love for us, God, who is rich in mercy, made us alive with Christ even when we were dead in transgressions—it is by grace you have been saved. And God raised us up with Christ and seated us with him in the heavenly realms in Christ Jesus, in order that in the coming ages he might show the incomparable riches of his grace, expressed in his kindness to us in Christ Jesus. For it is by grace you have been saved, through faith—and this is not from yourselves, it is the gift of God—not by works, so that no one can boast. For we are God's handiwork, created in Christ Jesus to do good works, which God prepared in advance for us to do" (Ephesians 2:1-10).

You used to be stuck, hopeless, and disobedient. But Paul doesn't say, "And then *you*…" No. It's "But then, *God*…" You were doomed, *but God* loved you so much that he gave you Jesus, raised you to life, seated you with him in the heavenly places as a trophy of his grace for all eternity, and invited you to join him in his mission.

Your story isn't about how amazing you are. It's about what Jesus did for you, and how your simple response to God has started changing you. It's about how God took your old life and gave you a new one; how God took your death and gave you life in trade; how you used to live for yourself but he gave you a mission worth dying for; how Jesus did all the work and gave you the credit for it. It's about how God gave you love, forgiveness, a new life, a position in heaven as his child, and security for all eternity.

Imagine being ten years old again, when a friend asks you what you got for Christmas. You wouldn't talk about the hot chocolate you drank, or how many times you went to the bathroom. Or if you did, your friend would interrupt you and ask, "But what did you *get?*" In the same way the point of your story isn't what you did, it's about the gift of life Jesus gave you. So point to him.

The second thing you should keep in mind when telling your story (or part of it) is to focus on what you have in common with the person you're sharing it with. Most Christians think they're supposed to make their story sound so amazing that it will be hard to resist. They do this by focusing on what makes their story unique, not realizing that a unique story might be fun to listen to, but hard to relate to.

The point of sharing your story is to help people realize they're just like you—and that what God did for you he can do for them, too. In fact, the best scenario is that while you're talking, that they begin to wonder if God is already doing that. Because he is.

NOW... RESPOND

Use the next few pages to write down some ideas for things you can share with others. Don't skip this! Do the work!

TELLING YOUR STORY

What are some "I used to…" issues in your life that God is starting to change? List them here.

What about those struggles are common to most *everyone?* IE, "I thought I could do it on my own because I like to think I have what it takes," etc. If you asked them, "Know what I mean?" they should be able to say, "Yeah, totally."

What were some of the realizations you came to about yourself, God, and Jesus in particular that helped you Believe in him?

How did God use other Believers to help you see the truth and respond to Jesus? What did they help you realize?

What has Jesus done for you? Why does this matter so much?

If there was one thing you'd like a close friend to know about Jesus, what would it be?

DAY THIRTY-ONE
Your Real Enemy

You have an enemy. No, not that jerk at the office. Believe it or not, Jesus wants you to love and pray for him (Matthew 5:44,45).

I'm talking about the devil, also called Satan, who commands legions of demons, "the spiritual forces of darkness in the heavenly realms" (Ephesians 6:12). Yes, he's real—and yes, it matters. A lot.

Lucifer, the name he used in the beginning, began as a cherubim (an angelic being) serving God. Because Satan and the demons are created beings, they aren't all-knowing. They aren't all-powerful. They can't be more than once place at once. They have limitations built into their identity just like people do. And they face the repercussions of rebellion against God just like people do.

Well, over time Lucifer became so impressed by his own splendour that he felt he should be exalted like God: "In the pride of your heart you say, "I am a god" (Ezekiel 28:2). He was able to dupe about a third of the angels in heaven to buy into his madness in rebellion against their Creator. As punishment, the whole works of them were cast out of heaven to wander as invisible beings in the spiritual realms overlapping the earth (See Revelation 12).

Since then, these 'fallen angels' have been called demons or evil / unclean spirits. Lucifer was renamed *satan* (lit., adversary or enemy) or the *devil* ('slanderer' or 'accuser'). Satan has declared war on people in general and Christians in particular as a way of trying to get some revenge on God. It was Satan way back in the garden of Eden who tempted Adam and Eve to sin against God. Here are a few verses where Jesus, who's seen the whole story, tells us what Satan is all about:

> "The devil... was a murderer from the beginning, not holding to the truth, for there is no truth in him. When he lies, he speaks his native language, for he is a liar and the father of lies" (John 8:44).

> He is "The thief (who) comes only to steal and kill and destroy" (John 10:10).

Satan is a murdering, lying, slandering, accusing, stealing enemy... who wants to ruin your life. He wants you to believe things that aren't true to hide the things that are. He wants to steal your hope, rob you of joy, deprive you of peace, and strip you of blessings so he can leave you discouraged, empty, and bitter. He wants to destroy your potential, ruin your relationships, and turn you into an agent of destruction in the lives of others.

That's the cold, hard truth.

I'm not trying to scare you. It's just vitally important to grasp this reality, "in order that Satan might not outwit us. For we are not unaware of his schemes" (I Corinthians 2:11).

John Eldredge, a Believer who writes and teaches about this kind of thing a lot, says, "the story of your life is the story of the long and brutal assault on your heart by the one that knows what you can become and fears it." That's so true.

Remember how God expelled Satan from heaven because of his pride? Well, that's because "God opposes the proud but shows favour to the humble." So when it comes to Satan, do you have to be afraid? Not at all. "Submit yourselves, then, to God," James says. Humble yourself and "resist the devil, and he will flee from you" (James 4:6,7). I can't wait to tell you more about that tomorrow!

> The main thing to know about Satan is this: never, ever agree with him about anything.

Because Satan is a liar, he and his demons spend a lot of their time slandering and accusing you. When you blow it, he'll plant ideas in your head like "I'm such a loser." When you're stressed out, he'll whisper, "You're never going to succeed." When others hurt you, he'll accuse and slander them: "She's such a stupid person."

Because Satan is a tempter, he will try to trick you into mistrusting God like he did with Adam and Eve. He'll tempt you to seek fulfillment outside of God's plan for you. He'll tempt you to act like he and his demons do—slandering people, putting them down, and dragging them down with you. When we treat people that way, we've unwittingly been doing the devil's work for him.

The main thing to know about Satan is this: never agree with him about anything. Never embrace his kind of thinking by saying, "You know, that's true. I am a loser." Never agree with him about others: "That guy is such a loser."

Reject Satan's lies and resist him as you submit to God and what he says about you (and others). If you don't, you'll end up playing for the wrong team and hurting yourself and others.

NOW... RESPOND

Take a few minutes to talk to God about your enemy. Ask the Holy Spirit to show you:

- If there are any lies, accusations, or slander you're believing about yourself that have been planted there by Satan
- If there are any lies, accusations, or slander you're believing about others that have been planted in your thinking by Satan

If something comes to mind—an idea about yourself or someone else that doesn't jive with what you've learned so far—confess to God you've been believing a lie, reject it, and ask him, "What's the truth to replace this lie?" Thank him for the truth and cling to that instead.

You'll be learning some powerful truths about dealing with Satan and his demons in tomorrow's reading.

DAY THIRTY-TWO
How to Deal with Satan and his Demons

I really hated to leave you hanging yesterday (thinking about Satan) without today's truth to balance it out. Sorry about that.

The truth is, in yourself you can't stand up to Satan. He and his demons are far more powerful than human beings will ever be. And how would you fight a demon, exactly? Stupid horror movies aside, what kind of gun could kill a spiritual being?

Good thing believing in Jesus gives us the life and power of Jesus. One time when he was on a boat trip with his disciples,

> When Jesus got out of the boat, a man with an evil spirit came to meet him… when he saw Jesus from a distance he ran and fell on his knees in front of him. He shouted at the top of his voice, "What do you want with me, Jesus, Son of the Most High God? Swear to me that you won't torture me!" For Jesus had said to him, "Come out of this man, you evil spirit!" Then Jesus asked him, "What is your name?" "My name is Legion," he replied, "for we are many." And he begged Jesus again and again not to send him out of the area. A large herd of pigs was feeding on the nearby hillside. The demons begged Jesus, "Send us among the pigs…" He gave them permission, and the evil spirits came out and went into the pigs. The herd, about two thousand in number, rushed down the steep bank into the lake and were drowned… When (the people) came to Jesus, they saw the man who had been possessed by demons, sitting there, dressed and in his right mind" (Mark 6:2,6-15).

You probably noticed this yourself, but I need to point it out. The demons—and there were many of them, maybe one for every pig—were deathly afraid of Jesus and were totally submitted to him. There was never a question about who was in charge or had the real power. And this was *before* Jesus died on the cross!

Paul wrote, "Having disarmed the powers and authorities, (Jesus) made a public spectacle of them, triumphing over them by the cross" (Colossians 2:14). As you put your faith in Christ, the Father shares Christ's victory with you, so that his win becomes your win: "He has rescued us from the dominion of darkness and brought us into the kingdom of the Son he loves" (Colossians 1:13).

What this means on a practical level is this: "In Christ all the fullness of the deity dwells in bodily form, and you have been given fullness in Christ, who is the head over every power and authority" (Colossians 2:9,10). When it comes to Satan and his demons, even all the power of hell, John writes, "You, dear children, are from God and have overcome them, because he who is in you (Jesus) is greater than he who is in the world (Satan)" (I John 4:4).

Here I need to explain the difference between power and authority. Power is the ability to do something; authority is the permission to use it. Christ has the power, and he shares that power with us by giving us his authority (permission) to use it. In Christ, you outrank every demon in the universe. You even outrank all of them put together. This is why, as you learned yesterday, as you "resist the devil... he will flee from you" (James 4:8).

There are two important points to make here. First of all, this means you never have to be afraid of the devil or any kind of evil. If anything, they are afraid of you realizing and acting on who you are in Christ. Demons have to submit to you because Jesus is in you.

Second, your authority to use Jesus' power against the devil puts you on the frontline of the battle to free humanity from the devil's bondage and death. "The reason the Son of God appeared was to destroy the work of the devil," Jesus explained. And then he sent us, his disciples, to be his witnesses by demonstrating his power and authority, shining his light in the dark where it's needed.

NOW... RESPOND

If you sense you are facing temptation, accusation, or something that belongs to the kingdom of darkness, apply these truths boldly. When you deal with evil, act and pray "in Jesus' name" (see day 37), not on your own strength. Look to Jesus for strength, then speak his authority out loud: "In the name of Jesus, I command these spirits of darkness to... " and deal with them accordingly.

If you sense someone else struggling with evil, stand up for them! This may sound freaky or strange, but it's how we stand against every spiritual enemy we face.

DAY THIRTY-THREE
Footholds and Strongholds

Before we move on to another topic, I need to spend some time helping you understand how Satan works to enslave us so you can work to avoid it. Like it or not, before you gave your life to Jesus, you belonged to Satan's kingdom of darkness:

> "You were dead in your transgressions and sins, in which you used to live when you followed the ways of this world and of the ruler of the kingdom of the air, the spirit who is now at work in those who are disobedient" (Ephesians 2:1-2).

But now you belong to God, "for he has rescued us from the dominion of darkness and brought us into the kingdom of the Son he loves" (Colossians 1:13).

Because you now belong to God—and because the devil isn't everywhere—he always works from the outside in. Most of the devil's influence in our lives goes unnoticed, even when he's doing profound damage. Either way, the only power he has in us is power he's tricked us into giving him. In other words, any work he's doing inside you is happening because you're letting him do it.

You've probably heard the phrase 'demon-possessed' before, or heard it come up in a movie somewhere. The way it's depicted is that demons enter a person and totally take over, to the point where the victim has no control over what's happening at all. Many Bible translations include the phrase 'demon possessed' in the New Testament.

The truth is far different. Drawing from Greek and Hebrew, the languages the Bible was originally written in, the more accurate translation is actually 'demonized.' This refers to a sliding scale of demonic influence ranging from what Paul would call a "foothold" (a little bit of influence) to what he calls a "stronghold" (a lot of influence). At no point, however, does a demon have full control over a person. No one can ever truthfully say, "The devil made me do it."

How does Satan gain footholds in our lives? And how does he build on them to create strongholds? Francis Frangipane's book, *The Three Battlegrounds*, does a good job of explaining this. Let me try to summarize.

The devil lurks in darkness. He's afraid of God's light. When he tempts us to sin and we give in, we have allowed some darkness to form within us. Satan then leverages that darkness as a *foothold* to create more darkness by tempting us into more sin. Think of each sin like a brick being laid in a wall between us and God in our own minds. As the wall grows, it begins to cast a shadow. A shadow is a kind of darkness where Satan can feel at home. A *stronghold*, Frangipane says, is a well-established area in our lives Satan has duped us into building (and defending!) against God.

Most of us would never knowingly allow Satan this kind of access or influence. So how does he do it? Well, remember, how Jesus called him "the Father of lies?" (John 8:44). That's because lies are *fathered*. He plants them within us, and as we accept them, they take on a life within us and grow like weeds, choking out the truths around it. Deception begins small, but it always grows. Unchecked, it will start to 'take over.'

Whenever we identify a lie, confess our sin and repent of it, we're taking a brick off the wall and giving Satan less to work with. When we surrender that stronghold to God, we're bringing it into his light for cleansing, demolition, and a new start. It's important to realize we always have the power and authority in Christ to reject Satan, all his footholds, and even his biggest strongholds in our lives. Jesus has disarmed him and we stand in Jesus. It's also important to note that while Satan may attach himself to certain issues in our lives, he's not living within us. Jesus is.

Because the devil isn't everywhere, he always works from the outside in.

That said, I want to briefly unpack three important areas the Bible flags as 'high risk' issues for believers in Christ—in other words, places where footholds and strongholds can grow quickly.

Anger & resentment. Paul says, "In your anger do not sin; Do not let the sun go down on your anger, and do not give the devil a foothold" (Ephesians 4:27). Getting angry isn't wrong; but if you let it fester, Satan reads that like raw meat attracts flies, and will use it as a foothold in your life. Review Day Twenty, "Forgiving Others" for more on this.

The Occult. The occult refers to any "supernatural, mystical, or magical beliefs, practices, or phenomena" not rooted in Christ and the One, true God. As God himself said to Moses,

> "Let no one be found among you who… practices divination or sorcery, interprets omens, engages in witchcraft, or casts spells, or who is a medium or spiritist or who consults the dead. Anyone who does these things is detestable to the Lord; because of these

same detestable practices the Lord your God will drive out those nations before you" (Deuteronomy 18:10-12).

Pretty clear, right? Don't use horoscopes, visit palm readers, read tarot cards, or visit mediums. They tap into the kingdom of darkness. Christ is now your "medium," and "in (him) are hidden all the treasures of wisdom" (insight into your life) "and knowledge"—everything you need to know. I tell you this, Paul says, "in order that no one may deceive you with fine sounding arguments," trying to convince you this stuff is okay for you (Colossians 2:3,4).

Sexual Sin. Sex and our sexuality are intensely spiritual, *not just physical.* This is why so many of the ancient pagan religions included temple prostitution and sex as part of their common rituals. Sex before marriage, prostitution, adultery, pornography, and all other perversions of God's gift of sex are all highly destructive and give the devil footholds in our lives. This is why Paul wrote,

> "Flee from sexual immorality... do you not know that your body is a Temple of the Holy Spirit, who is in you, whom you have received from God? You are not your own; you were bought with a price. Therefore honour God with your body" (I Corinthians 6:18-20).

NOW... RESPOND

The concepts you've learned today are massively important. Take some time to pray about them, and ask God to show you if you have unwittingly allowed Satan a foothold (or even a stronghold) in your life. If a foothold is revealed, confess it and repent. If a stronghold is revealed, find another Believer to help you process how to destroy it and find freedom in Christ.

DAY THIRTY-FOUR
Fulness in Christ

On Day 14 you learned that as a child of God you are the place where God's kingdom comes, where the virtues and power of heaven take on shape and touch this world for the better. The entire flow of God's kingdom is now *towards* you because he wants His life to flow into and *through* you. Christ is the Vine and you are a branch on that Vine, where the fruit of Jesus can manifest in and through your life.

Nothing can compare to those moments when God uses you to manifest a slice of heaven here on earth. Let me unpack something that will help position you to be used by God in incredible ways .

If you own a retro stereo system, it may actually have a few dials instead of buttons or touch-screens. Your life is like one of those dials, with two possible settings:

Give  **Get**

In any given moment your heart is either set to *give* something or to *get* something. If your heart is set on *give*, you're postured to let heaven flow into and through you. But if your heart is set on *get*, you've reversed the flow; you're looking to someone or something other than God to fill you. You're trying to suck things into yourself instead of giving things away. The flow of heaven stops cold.

Human beings are born selfish and sinful. We're *set on get* right out of the box (Psalm 51:5). Most of us know that being totally selfish is a bad thing, so we try to set the dial somewhere *between give* and *get*, maybe a little more towards the *give* side:

Give  **Get**

In other words, we like to give… if we get a little something in return. I give you a hug, maybe, because I know you'll give me one back. The truth is, that's being set on *get* while trying to look like I'm set on *give*. Which is not, I hope you're seeing, the same thing.

So how do we set our hearts on *give*? Is it even possible?

Yes! But the only way you can set your heart on *give* is to believe Jesus has either *met your* needs, is *meeting* your needs, or *will* meet your needs in the future. This frees you from having to get what you need from me or anyone else. You don't need to *get* something from anyone because you already *have* what you need. This is the only way to truly and fully love someone.

Remember how your "new self (is) created to be like God in true righteousness" (Ephesians 4:24)? Well, "God is love'" (I John 4:8), so the new you is loving—*set on give*—like He is. The new you is free from manipulating others to get what you need because you have already been given "every spiritual blessing in Christ" (Ephesians 1:3). The new you knows "his divine power has given us everything we need for a godly life through our knowledge of him who called us by his own glory and goodness" (II Peter 1:3).

As you understand and accept that you've been rooted and established in the love of God, you'll realize: not only are your needs met, you're overflowing with *more* than you'll ever need. The Holy Spirit is an eternal spring of living water flowing from within you (John 7:38). God is constantly completing you and giving you what others need. He wants you to learn to believe this heart and soul, living your life set on *give*, passing on his grace and truth as he leads and guides you.

NOW... RESPOND

Ask God to show you where you've been setting your heart: *Give, get,* or living in denial somewhere in between. Confess that to him and receive his forgiveness and grace.

Ask him, by the power of His Spirit, to convince you of your fulness in Christ. Reflect on imagery that helps reinforce these truths: You are a branch, filled with the life of the vine, and grapes are coming out of you. You're a well, overflowing with the water of the Holy Spirit. Do this often. When you meet people, ask God to flow through you to love them and meet their needs. Then go for it!

DAY THIRTY-FIVE
Gifted

One of the most profound images in the New Testament is this:

"Just as each of us has one body with many members, and these
members do not all have the same function, so in Christ we, though
many, form one body, and each member belongs to all the
others" (Romans 12:4,5).

Which *body* is he talking about? "The body of Christ, and each one of
you is a part of it" (I Corinthians 12:27).

Jesus lives in you, but you're just one small and incomplete expression
of who Jesus is. Collectively, Believers in Jesus form Christ's spiritual body,
so that he is more fully expressed through us.

When we work together,

"We will grow to become in every respect the mature body of
him who is the head, that is, Christ. From him the whole body,
joined and held together by every supporting ligament, grows and
builds itself up in love, as each part does its work" (Ephesians
4:15,16).

It's like this: Jesus' Holy Spirit gives each one of us a function in his
spiritual body by manifesting a piece of himself through us. This is our
role to play in building the Church. The empowerment we receive to fulfill
this role (or roles) is called a *spiritual gift*.

Because we all have different functions in Christ's body, *"we* have
different gifts, according to the grace given to each of us" (I Corinthians
12:6). God can use you in lots of different ways, not just through your gift
—so maybe think of your gift or gifts as God's favourite way(s) of using
you.

Paul's advice?

"If your gift is prophesying, then prophesy in accordance with
your faith; if it is serving, then serve; if it is teaching, then teach; if
it is to encourage, then give encouragement; if it is giving, then
give generously; if it is to lead, do it diligently; if it is to show
mercy, do it cheerfully" (I Corinthians 12:7,8).

This isn't an exhaustive list. Other gifts listed in the New Testament include healing, miracles, speaking in tongues, interpreting tongues, words of knowledge, discerning of spirits, and hospitality. This list isn't exhaustive either.

Some gifts are more public and splashy, while others are more behind the scenes. All of them are essential parts of Christ's work in the world, so "the eye cannot say to the hand, "I don't need you!" And the head cannot say to the feet, "I don't need you!" On the contrary, those parts of the body that seem to be weaker are indispensable" (I Corinthians 12:21,22). "All these are the work of one and the same Spirit, and he distributes them to each one, just as he determines" (I Corinthians 12:11).

The best way to discover your place in Christ's body (your gifts) is to jump in, try stuff, grow up in your faith, and pay attention to how God tends to use you over time. In other words, if people are regularly encouraged in their faith by being with you, that might be your gift. If people tend to get healed more often when you pray than when other people pray, you might have the gift of healing. The point isn't to give yourself a label or put yourself in a box, but to figure out your role so when you see that role is needed, you can step in and help with the Holy Spirit's help.

NOW... RESPOND

Study I Corinthians 12 in the New Testament, praying as you go. If you need a refresher on how to study the Bible you can re-read days 16-18.

Reflect on your life in Jesus so far. Have you noticed God using you to help people since you put your faith in Christ? If so, how? Make note of this and see if there is a pattern developing.

Maybe you haven't been helping people yet because you've been focused on growing your own faith. Growing your faith is important, but you need to invest in others to keep that up. You don't have to be very good at it, just start figuring out how to love people and see what happens.

DAY THIRTY-SIX
Serving Your King

God describes himself many different ways: He is Father, Creator, Saviour, and dozens more. What some people miss is that a lot of these names imply a parallel identity for you and me:

- God is Father, so we are his children.
- God is Creator, so we are his creations.
- God is Teacher, we are his disciples.
- God is like a Vine, and we are the branches.
- God is a Shepherd, and we are his sheep.

God is too gloriously infinite for a single metaphor to contain all of who he is (and who or what that makes us). Every one of these pairs is another facet of life to explore and enjoy. Today we're going to explore the fact that God is our Lord and King, and we are his servants.

One day when Jesus and his disciples arrived at a home to spend some time together, Jesus got down on his knees and began washing their feet—something the household servant was supposed to do when the guests arrived (this was the custom in those days). When he was done, Jesus turned to his disciples and said,

> "You call me 'Teacher' and 'Lord,' and rightly so, for that is what I am. Now that I, your Lord and Teacher, have washed your feet, you also should wash one another's feet. I have set you an example that you should do as I have done for you. Very truly I tell you, no servant is greater than his master, nor is a messenger greater than the one who sent him. Now that you know these things, you will be blessed if you do them" (John 13:13-17)

Some people miss the point of the passage, focusing on washing feet in particular. But the real point is this: If he, the Son of God, "did not come to be served, but to serve, and to give his life as a ransom for many" (Mark 10:45), then we should follow his example by living—and dying, if necessary—to serve others.

The second point is just as powerful: How do we serve God? By serving people:

"Anyone who loves their life will lose it, while anyone who hates their life in this world will keep it for eternal life. Whoever serves me must follow me; and where I am, my servant also will be. My Father will honour the one who serves me" (John 12:25,26).

"If you have any encouragement from being united with Christ, if any comfort from his love, if any common sharing in the Spirit, if any tenderness and compassion, then make my joy complete by being like-minded, having the same love, being one in spirit and of one mind. Do nothing out of selfish ambition or vain conceit. Rather, in humility value others above yourselves, not looking to your own interests but each of you to the interests of the others" (Philippians 2:1-5).

Being a servant doesn't mean being a doormat or letting people use and abuse you. There is a difference between giving and letting people take. Living as a servant means laying down your pride to put others' needs above your own. It means choosing to be inconvenienced when someone needs your help. It means sharing time, money, possessions, energy, and relationships to bless others when they need a hand.

NOW... RESPOND

Everywhere you look, people have needs. You can't possibly meet all of them. Nor should you try. On the other hand, your life should be about helping people. So where do you start? Well, if you're a servant of God, it means you're at his disposal. So pray, "Lord, how do you want to spend me today?"

And then, just go about your business. Once you get used to praying this kind of prayer, you'll notice God putting needs and people in your path for you to serve. Heads up—these opportunities will probably feel like inconveniences in the moment. But dive in anyway, and get busy helping.

DAY THIRTY-SEVEN
Generosity

If you stop to think about it, God is the most generous Being in the universe.

For starters, he created this world for us to live in free of charge. He then filled it with beauty and richness for us to enjoy and use for our own development and thriving.

When turned from him to make life work on our own, spiralling into sin, death, and darkness, he sent leaders to try and guide us back on track. He sent prophets to warn us about the consequences of our actions. And he finally sent his Son, Jesus, to pay for our sins, rise from the dead, and give us the credit for it all.

Paul's advice? "Follow God's example, therefore, as dearly loved children and walk in the way of love, just as Christ loved us and gave himself up for us" (Ephesians 5:1).

In the broadest sense, generosity is far more than giving money to someone. Generosity is love in action. God calls us to be generous with words of encouragement, time, friendships, patience, forgiveness, our possessions, and yes, our money.

I know that there are churches out there that take advantage of weak minded people and their naive generosity—but the fact is, God commands us to be generous people just as he is a generous God. The New Testament has more to say about how we handle money than almost any other issue. Why is money such a big deal?

"No one can serve two masters," Jesus said. "Either you will hate the one and love the other, or you will be devoted to the one and despise the other. You cannot serve both God and money" (Matthew 6:24). Jesus knew the power greed can hold in the human heart, and money is directly tied to greed. It can become an idol, a kind of 'god' we serve and worship by giving our energy to making more of it and keeping it to ourselves. He also knew that the only antidote for greed was generosity.

You might be thinking, "Oh, but I don't have very much money." But the amount isn't the problem. It's how much you want what you have and what you'll do to get more. And just like greed isn't about being rich, neither is generosity. In II Corinthians chapter 8, Paul is writing the Corinthian believers about some amazing Believers:

"They gave as much as they were able, and even beyond their ability. Entirely on their own, they urgently pleaded with us for the privilege of sharing in this service to the Lord's people. And they exceeded our expectations: They gave themselves first of all to the Lord, and then by the will of God also to us" (II Corinthians 8:3-5).

Awesome! They understood what we need to learn: Giving to his work (which includes Church) is giving to God. He goes on to say,

Each of you should give what you have decided in your heart to give, not reluctantly or under compulsion, for God loves a cheerful giver. And God is able to bless you abundantly, so that in all things at all times, having all that you need, you will abound in every good work…You will be enriched in every way so that you can be generous on every occasion, and through us your generosity will result in thanksgiving to God" (II Corinthians 9:6-8,11).

Did you catch that? God wants you to be generous—and the more generous you are, the more he'll give you to give away!

All this to say, giving to God by giving to Church is an important part of being a disciple of Jesus.

How much should you give? In the Old Testament, God's people were commanded to give ten percent of their income to God. In the New Testament, the rule is, "be generous, and be cheerful about it." It's not about percentages, it's about the heart. Personally, our family uses ten percent as a benchmark, and then the more God blesses us, the more we give away, both to Church and to needs people have all around us.

NOW... RESPOND

Start giving to your home church this coming Sunday. Trust that when you put God first, God will take not only take care of you, but help you to become more and more generous as time goes on. Trust me, it's fun to bless other people by helping out!

DAY THIRTY-EIGHT
Miracles

You've been learning that as a disciple of Jesus, you are the place where God's "as it is in heaven" takes shape "on earth."

I hope you're starting to see that this is probably the most exciting thing you'll ever hear, because it means God can use you to do amazing things. Supernatural things. Miraculous things!

"Oh, I could never do that," you might be thinking. "I don't have enough faith." And you're partly right. You never could, on your own—but listen to what Jesus has to say about that:

> "The Apostles said to the Lord, "Increase our faith!" He replied, "If you have faith as small as a mustard seed, you can say to this mulberry tree, 'Be uprooted and planted in the sea,' and it will obey you" (Luke 17:5,6).

Crazy, right? But this isn't about mulberry trees, it's about faith. Not faith in yourself, faith in God. In the power of Jesus. In Day thirty-four, you learned that when we set our hearts on *giving* instead of *getting*, we align ourselves with the flow of heaven so that God both fills us and overflows from us into others.

You don't have to be super-spiritual or a veteran Christian for this to work. It's not about you, it's about God loving the world so much that he gave us Jesus. It's about Jesus loving the people around you so much that he keeps on giving himself to the world. The supreme privilege of your life is to offer yourself as a channel he can flow through.

In the name of Jesus, I have seen a weird growth fall off my son's back after praying for him for a few days. I've seen tendonitis healed, migraines cut off, a cripple start walking, a rash disappear in moments, a dislocated shoulder pop itself in place, and even an irregular heartbeat steady itself in a few seconds. And that's just the tip of the iceberg!

What you need to realize is, because Jesus lives in you, anything can happen through you at any time. The impact you can have on others isn't limited by your gifts, by your abilities, your intelligence, or your life-experience. It's limited only by your faith—your confidence in Jesus' love for people you meet and his ability to do the impossible to help them. This is why Paul wrote,

"I pray that you, being rooted and established in love, may have power, together with all the Lord's holy people, to grasp how wide and long and high and deep is the love of Christ…that you may be filled to the measure of all the fullness of God" (Ephesians 3:17-19)

Why is grasping God's boundless love so important? Because he "is able to do immeasurably more than all we ask or imagine, according to his power that is at work within us" (Ephesians 3:20). His power within us, within you, can do more than you could ever ask or even imagine. Imagine *that!*

Or maybe you can't imagine. So let me explain what I do to help you visualize it a little bit. Let's say I see someone walking with a limp.

First, I listen for God's leading. If I feel an inner sense that I need to pray for them, I work up the courage (yes, I'm often afraid too!) and approach them to talk.

> As a disciple of Jesus, you are the place where God's "as it is in heaven" takes shape "on earth."

Next, I ask them about what's wrong. So I'd say, "Hey, I noticed you limping there. Did you hurt your leg?" In the next few moments, their response will determine whether I follow through or not. If they brush me off, I generally leave it be. If they tell me what happened, I take the time to really listen and sympathize with them.

Let's say the guy says, "Yeah, I blew out my knee playing basketball last week."

"Oh, that sucks," I might say. "Is it really painful?"

"Oh yeah," they reply. "Really painful."

"When does it hurt the most?" I ask. I'm trying to find out where it hurts and what *motion* makes it hurt. You'll see why next.

"When I bend it like this, it hurts like crazy. And I can't really flex it further than that."

"Ouch. That must be hard." This is where I ask them, "Hey, can I pray for you? I've seen God do some crazy stuff." By the way, I'm praying in my mind through this whole conversation, thanking God for loving this guy and asking him to reveal his glory to him through me.

Usually when I ask if I can pray, they shrug their shoulders awkwardly, and say, "Sure, why not," or something like that. I've only had one person turn me down (If you get turned down, don't take it personally. The point is to love them, not to accomplish some kind of mission on them).

Now for the prayer. I usually take a second or two to calm myself and turn my attention totally to God. Here is how I often pray:

"Father, thank you that you're here with us, and that you give us your Spirit. Holy Spirit, thank you that you bring us the love and power of Jesus. Would you please flow into "Bob" right now and heal his knee? In Jesus' name, thank you."

But I'm not done. I've asked God to do what only he can do, and now I need to step out in faith and tell the "mulberry bush" to move. This is when I take what the guy has described to me and combine it with what I sense God leading me to say:

"Okay, knee, in the name of Jesus, be totally healed. Tendons, tighten up! Inflammation, dissolve in Jesus' name. And all pain, go now in the name of Jesus."

As I'm doing this, I'm visualizing God's power coming into the injury I'm praying for and totally healing it. I 'see' the person well, smiling, and amazed in my minds' eye (by faith, of course), and praising God with me.

When I'm done I stop praying and ask the person how they're doing. "Any change?" I might ask. "Try doing what was causing you pain just a minute ago." See, I'm not trying to trick them. If there's no change, I don't want them to pretend there is.

They may be healed, but often they'll feel a bit better. Sometimes they may not feel any different at all. Don't panic! It's common for me to pray for someone at twice. If you ask them what's changed, they might say, "Huh. Wow. It doesn't hurt as much, but it's still really stiff over here."

Then I say, "Wow, thank you Jesus." And then I go through these 'steps' again, focusing on what still needs a touch from God.

Lots of people wonder, "What if nothing happens when I pray?" Well, first of all, most people aren't expecting it to work, so they're not exactly going to be crushed with disappointment. But regardless of how things turn out, I make sure to affirm God's love for them. "Hey, God really loves you. That's why I prayed for you."

I pray for my immediate family all the time. I think of them as practice (not for God, because he doesn't need practice) for me and my boldness. My advice? No matter how things turn out, keep praying. Keep doing it. And see where it goes.

NOW... RESPOND

Does this sound scary to you? That's normal! Here's my advice: The verse I quoted earlier talked about what we *ask* and what we *imagine*. So first, ask God to use you to heal people and to give you the boldness to reach out.

Next, prepare for what God might want to do by imagining him doing it through you. Imagine yourself doing what I did.

First, though…

- Imagine being brushed off when you ask about what's wrong. Imagine yourself not only surviving, but being totally fine with it.
- Imagine asking if you can pray, and them declining. Imagine smiling, and saying, "Well, God loves you. Have a great day," and walking away, totally okay with yourself.
- Imagine praying and commanding, and nothing happens. Imagine the person thanking you for praying, and you affirming God's love for them anyway.

But also…

- Imagine getting over your fear by initiating the conversation.
- Imagine them telling you what's wrong.
- Imagine God's peace settling over you.
- Imagine yourself asking them if you can pray.
- Imagine them saying, "Uh, sure. I guess."
- Imagine praying the prayer you might pray.
- Imagine commanding what's wrong to be right.
- Imagine their eyes widening in amazement as their pain leaves.
- Imagine praising God together for showing his love through a miracle!

There is no doubt in my mind that God wants to use you to manifest glimpses of heaven on earth, and even more than that.

DAY THIRTY-NINE
Dealing with Conflict

If you haven't figured it out by now, the Church is full of hypocritical, moody, imperfect, annoying people…

… just like you.

We're called disciples because we're still learning and always will be. We're a crazy, sinful mess—that's why Jesus had to rescue us. If you haven't been hurt by Christians in your church yet, you don't know them well enough. When new people come into our Life Group, I often tell them straight up: "We're going to hurt you. It won't be on purpose, but it will happen. We're a big, dysfunctional family learning live from our new selves in Christ—and many days, we'll get it wrong. But then again, you'll also hurt us."

This is why Paul writes,

"As God's chosen people, holy and dearly loved, clothe yourselves with compassion, kindness, humility, gentleness and patience. Bear with each other and forgive one another if any of you has a grievance against someone. Forgive as the Lord forgave you. And over all these virtues put on love, which binds them all together in perfect unity" (Colossians 3:12-14).

How do you handle conflict when it happens? What do you do when a fellow believer hurts you? If love can't cover it—in other words, if it still bugs you after you've forgiven them and it's put a strain on your relationship, Jesus points the way:

"If your brother or sister sins against you, go and point out their fault, just between the two of you. If they listen to you, you have won them over. But if they will not listen, take one or two others along, so that 'every matter may be established by the testimony of two or three witnesses.' If they still refuse to listen, tell it to the church; and if they refuse to listen even to the church, treat them as you would a pagan or a tax collector" (Matthew 18:15-17).

When someone hurts you (unless it's a case of abuse or you're afraid for your safety), don't talk to someone else *about* them. That's what kids call tattling. It's what adults call gossip or slander. So talk to the offender *directly*. Give them a chance to apologize and /or explain themselves. This alone would disarm most conflicts before they have a chance to escalate and cause more damage. If you can't find a way to restore what's broken in the relationship, you can pull in a neutral party—not to prove you right, but to help you fix what's broken.

If things can't be fixed, if the person who's hurt you won't repent—won't say sorry—treat them like you would someone who doesn't know Jesus. In other words, love them anyway, because they obviously don't understand grace.

What if you're the person who did something wrong or hurt someone else? Don't wait for them to confront you. Go to them and apologize. Ask for forgiveness. Make it right (Matthew 5:23,24).

What if someone comes to you to talk about another person who's hurt or offended them? You play an important role! The first question you should ask is, "Have you talked to them about it?" If they haven't, gently say, "I think that's the first thing you should do. If you talk to them and it doesn't work out, maybe I can help you guys work this out." Don't listen to their complaint, or you'll be enabling gossip to spread in the church. Gossip needs ears to survive.

Life is messy. Good thing Jesus shows us that his family is built on forgiveness, forgiveness he bought and paid for with his own blood.

NOW... RESPOND

Is there anyone that's hurt you that you've tried to forgive? Ask God to show you if you should follow these steps to help resolve the issue.

Have you hurt or offended someone? Go, humble yourself and apologize. Make it right.

DAY FORTY
Dealing With Idols in Your Own Heart

There's a reason the first and greatest commandment in the Bible is to love God with all our heart, soul, mind, and strength. Simply put, the root of all sin is worshipping something other than God. When we're trusting in, looking to, celebrating, and submitting to anything or anyone but God for what only he can provide, everything goes to pot.

From the very beginning, people have been trying to exalt themselves as the captains of their own fates. Paul says,

> "Although they claimed to be wise, they became fools and *exchanged* the glory of the immortal God for images made to look like a mortal human being and birds and animals and reptiles... They *exchanged* the truth about God for a lie, and worshiped and served created things rather than the Creator" (Romans 1:22,23,25).

Whenever we exchange God for someone or something else, we've turned our inner world upside down. Look what happens when we get our worship screwed up; immediately after the previous verses, Paul goes on:

> "Therefore God gave them over in the sinful desires of their hearts to sexual impurity for the degrading of their bodies with one another... Even their women exchanged natural sexual relations for unnatural ones. In the same way the men also abandoned natural relations with women and were inflamed with lust for one another... God gave them over to a depraved mind, so that they do what ought not to be done. They have become filled with every kind of wickedness, evil, greed and depravity. They are full of envy, murder, strife, deceit and malice. They are gossips, slanderers, God-haters, insolent, arrogant and boastful; they invent ways of doing evil; they disobey their parents; they have no understanding, no fidelity, no love, no mercy" (Romans 1:24,26-31).

When we look to God, who is loving, merciful, true, beautiful, patient, and kind, our lives slowly take on his character. *We become like who or what we worship.* When we look to lesser things, our lives become less than God intended. Always.

Worship of other gods is called idolatry throughout the Bible. This obviously refers to worshipping physical idols, like some religions of the world still practice. But idolatry also refers to whatever we give a place higher than God in our lives.

Jesus is the King of Kings; he bows to no one. But when we start looking to people to satisfy our longing for affirmation, love, and wholeness, we're 'bowing' to them as if they are the ultimate Source of our happiness. When we throw all our energy into making money, we're 'bowing' to money and greed as if it could truly satisfy us.

Most people don't worship satan directly. Most of our idolatry is more subtle than that. Knowing this, Paul says, "Put to death, therefore, whatever belongs to your earthly nature: sexual immorality, impurity, lust, evil desires and greed, which is idolatry" (Colossians 3:5,6).

God uses all kinds of people and things to meet our needs. In fact, "every good and perfect gift is from above, coming down from the Father of the heavenly lights" (James 1:17). The problem begins when "we make *good* things *god* things," as someone has said. We look to the gift instead of the Giver, who is ultimately God.

NOW... RESPOND

For starters, ask yourself (and God) the following question to uncover idols you may be worshipping without knowing it: Is there something or someone I'm trusting to give me what only God can provide—like my sense of validation, security, identity, or worth?

When you realize you have been trusting in an idol, it's not enough to just say, "oops," or "sorry." Confess it as a sin to God:

"God, I've been looking to _____ to try and get my sense of _____. This is sin because I've exchanged you for an idol that can't satisfy me. I reject this false god and I put my trust in you and worship you instead, Lord Jesus. Please help me keep my heart and mind fixed on you. Amen."

WHAT'S NEXT?
Recap and Next Steps

Wow, you're done! The purpose of this book was to give you a forty day head start in your new faith in Jesus.

I hope and pray several things have happened as a result of reading and praying though this material:

- That you've learned to look to Jesus as a way of life
- That you've learned how to respond to him when he initiates things in your life
- That you've begun to understand some basic concepts that will help you become a better follower and lover of Jesus

If you can give a "thumbs up" on these three things, that would be gold. But on a really practical level, I also hope you:

- Have joined a Life Group to help you give shape to your discipleship to Jesus
- Have gotten baptized
- Are starting to lean into your new lifestyle of sharing the love and truth of Jesus with others
- Have started studying the Bible for yourself
- Have started giving regularly towards the Manifest mission

There are a couple of things you could do next to help you grow in your faith from here on in:

- Pick up a *Disciple's Guide* at the Welcome Centre. It will help you go deeper as a disciple and teach you how to help other people become disciples of Jesus. And it's free like this book is!
- Dive into some of the other books at the Welcome Centre: *Beloved, Go With the Flow,* and *Realms.*

I can't think of a better "Now What?" to give you from here than what the Apostle Paul wrote to some new Believers I'm I'm here knew:

"So then, just as you received Christ Jesus as Lord, continue to live your lives in him, rooted and built up in him, strengthened in the faith as you were taught, and overflowing with thankfulness" (Colossians 2:6).

Well, that's it for now! Remember, Jesus is enough and you belong to him!

BRAD
HUEBERT

25584345R00059

Made in the USA
Middletown, DE
04 November 2015